YOGA AND LONG LIFE

BY

YOGI GUPTA

DODD, MEAD AND COMPANY

NEW YORK

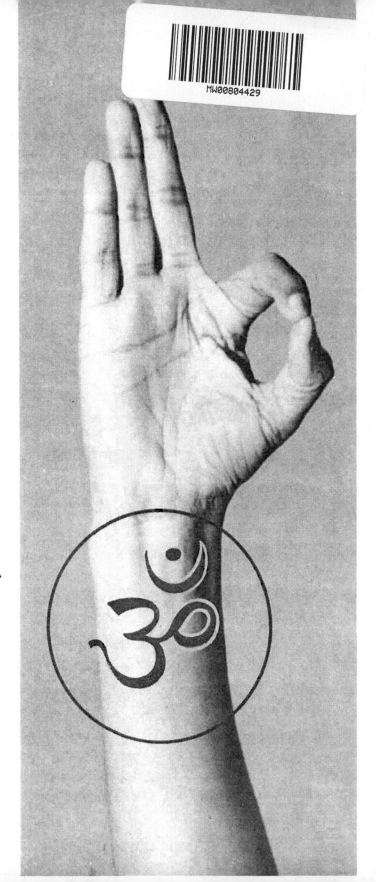

To my students of the United States of America,

especially those of New York, who encouraged me

to write this book and who financed its publication

Yoga
and
Long
Life

The meaning and significance of the pose of the Author's hand, and of the symbol on his wrist, which are shown on the Cover and on the Title Page

The pose is *Jnana-Mudra* (symbol of knowledge). It is used in meditative poses, and in various Hatha Yoga postures, as a way of locking the vibrations into the body.

The three extended fingers (middle, ring and last finger) symbolize the three states of life: Creation, Preservation and Transmutation. The circle, which is formed by the joining of the thumb and the tip of the index finger, symbolizes the union of individual will with the Cosmic, or Divine, Will.

The symbol on the author's wrist means OM (pronounced: A-U-M). To the Yogis, it is considered a sacred word, since it represents the sum-total of all sound vibrations in the entire Universe. (Ah — the guttural or root sound; Oh — roof of the mouth or middle sound; Ma — the labial or final sound). Correct pronunciation of the word OM stirs up the latent faculties lying dormant in the nerve centers. Meditation on OM leads to spiritual awakening.

INTRODUCTION

by K. FOX, *A Director*

of The Yoga Foundation of America

Yogi Gupta was born at Kanpur, United Provinces, North India, into an aristocratic and well-to-do family. As a youth he studied law and was admitted to the Bar. He practiced before one of the high courts of India and although his legal career was dedicated to the service of humanity it left him dissatisfied. He therefore decided to study Yoga. He was initiated into the Holy Order of Sanyasa (ordained monk) in Benares and thereafter continued practicing Karma Yoga (Yoga of action and selfless service) and Hatha Yoga under the personal guidance of Swami Sivananda Jee Maharaj, Chancellor of the Yoga Vedanta Forest University, and Founder-President of the Divine Life Society (India). At present Dr. Gupta is the President of the Kailashananda Mission, in Rishikesh, Himalayas, India, surrounded by the Himalayan peaks, and on the banks of the holy river Ganges. He is also Founder of the recently organized Yoga Foundation of America. At these institutions and elsewhere many people have been helped to health and youthful vitality under his guidance.

It is Yogi Gupta's thesis that through the practice of Yoga, for as little as fifteen minutes daily, the useful life-span of people can be greatly increased. By increasing the body's powers of resistance, he claims that the practitioner of Yoga exercises can ward off many common diseases. Yogi Gupta's work in the United States has produced remarkable results.

He is most practical. According to him, life is a rare opportunity to perfect oneself. Perfection of one's body, mind and soul is necessary to make oneself useful to one's country and to humanity in general and to find one's personal salvation. To him service to humanity ('God in man') is the greatest thing one may do with his life.

In order to prepare himself for this service, and prior to being initiated into the Yogic Order, Yogi Gupta spent many isolated years in

5

fasting, prayer, penance and meditation in a Himalayan valley. The benefits he received from his Yoga disciplines increased his faith in the various religions of the world which. advocate fasting, prayer and pilgrimages — it is said that visiting holy lands and places is a strong factor in self-purification. In Yogi Gupta's case the place he selected for further penance and meditation during his pilgrimage through India was in Mount Rishikesh in the Himalayas. This place is famous for saints and sages, and is called *Muni Ki Reti* (Place of Saints and Sages).

Nowadays Yogi Gupta fasts and prays when he is tense or in need of inspiration and courage to fulfill his mission. His love towards human beings is great. "Simple living and high thinking" is one of his mottos in life.

Equally important to him is *service* to humanity. He believes there is nothing greater a man may do than to teach his fellows how they may live a healthy, pure and happy life, both in thought and action.

Yogi Gupta himself is a complete vegetarian. He never eats anything which has come in contact with fire at any time, nor does he eat dairy products such as milk and cheese, or eggs. He does not add salt to his diet, nor does he drink coffee or tea. However, he never exhorts his audiences or students to keep to a similar diet. "To adapt, aujust and accommodate, in different, adverse circumstances" is a part of his philosophy. One should not find fault with others, he says; by cultivating the above virtues one should establish a more harmonious relationship with other people. He never discourages those who are non-vegetarian from practicing Yoga. He claims that as long as one eats in moderation, one can improve one's health.

To achieve perfection in body and mind he tells his students that they should not develop the habit of becoming a slave to anything. Slavery to food, vegetarian or non-vegetarian, when one must have a particular thing to eat at a particular hour, will only delay the time of a person's perfection. This simple philosophy, and his easy techniques of Yoga exercises and breathing, and system of nutrition, which seems suited to the West, will make his teachings practical and inspiring to the people of this country.

K. Fox

AUTHOR'S

PREFACE

When I was invited to speak at a Health Convention held at the Morrison Hotel, Chicago, in August 1954, I had a difficult decision to make. Although it is the duty of a yogi to make his knowledge available to whomsoever may seek it, irrespective of caste, creed or nationality, I had doubts whether I could come. My time was already so overtaxed directing the Yoga Health Sanatorium in the Himalayas, near Kashmir, besides editing the monthly journal published by the Yoga Vedanta Forest University that I had brought to an end my regular course of lectures at the latter place and also had been regretfully compelled to withhold admission to several *sadhaka-s* (seekers) both from India and abroad.

And there was yet another difficulty. I had promised my own *guru* (teacher) that I would go forth into the world as a missionary, should he so request me, on the completion of my studies and therefore, I contacted him.

He said: "On the very first day you joined us I told you that we had a mission to do. You promised me that on the completion of your training, and should the opportunity arise, you would go forth into the world as a missionary. That opportunity you have now, Swami Kailashananda Jee Maharaj.[1] You have received full training in the nine different forms of yoga[2] and now the time has come for you to go abroad and teach those in poor health and an unhappy state of mind how to regain their lost health and happiness."

"Do you think," I asked my *guru*, "I will succeed in maintaining my principles and abiding by your teachings in the busy western world where temptations and the noise of industrial life may overwhelm me, when I am used to the peaceful atmosphere of this ashram (monastery)?"

---

[1] The name given to me when I was ordained a *Swami* (monk)

[2] These are explained on p 25.

"After your training here, your penances and your fasting, your long pilgrimages, nothing will distract you," my *guru* replied. "You will hold your head high like the hoary Himalayas themselves, among all the distractions of the cities of the West. Go forth, my son, since there are many who will want to listen to you."

After receiving the blessing of my teacher, I returned to my sanatorium, and leaving it in the care of my colleagues until my return, I arrived in Chicago for the Health Convention. At this convention I was not quite prepared for the immense interest shown by the people who heard my several talks. I was invited by various organizations to speak in cities all over the U.S.A., and I was given opportunities to reach mass audiences through television networks. And finally I was persuaded by my friends to become president of the Yoga Foundation of America. I could not resist the interest of the American people (which is continually growing). It is this fact which has made me decide to stay on in this country.

YOGI GUPTA

CONTENTS

PART FIVE

ILLUSTRATIONS

FIGURES

Illustration 1. Yogi Gupta

Part One

1. YOGA IS A SCIENCE

Yoga is a science of living, and those who practice it are known as Yogis. Yoga has nothing to do with any particular caste, religion, or nation, and is therefore universally applicable and useful. Yoga sets up no particular God, or gods; neither does it deny the existence of God. It is a system of physical and thought culture. One may be a Jew, Moslem, Buddhist, Hindu, Christian or atheist and still be a student of Yoga, since it neither criticizes any religion, nor does it support one particular religion. Some Yogis may not recognize supernatural powers or the duty of man to owe allegiance to them. Still they may reach *self-realization* through *self-knowledge* by the practice of Yoga, besides the attainment of miraculous powers, such as perfect control of the mind and body, including even the involuntary organs of the body. As defined in the Oxford English Dictionary, Yoga is "a system of philosophic meditation and asceticism designed to effect the reunion of the soul with the universal spirit." This is true of certain forms of Yoga which are inextricably mixed in Hindu metaphysics, and, in a sense, it is true of Hatha Yoga, which is the subject of this book. However, the average student need not concern himself overmuch with this definition, and it is for him I have written this book. It should be sufficient for him to know that Yoga is a system of mental and physical training with prescribed postures, breathing exercises, meditation and relaxation.

Although yogic exercises may be compared to physical culture exercises, they differ from them in many ways. They are not intended for the development of large muscles, as in physical culture. Nor are they aimed at merely disciplining the body. Yoga disciplines the *mind* as well as the body. The exercises of Yoga stand unparalleled among all the systems of physical exercises, because of the benefits they have to offer, a fact which the West has but too tardily grasped. Now that the knowledge of the East is being systematized and presented along Western lines, the West has become more receptive than before, and

15

has even attempted to adapt it to her own needs in physical culture, and in medicine, dieting and nutrition. It is my belief that this century will bring about a closer understanding between the East and the West.

Yoga teaches in easy, simple steps the control of the mind, its thought, and the whole body itself, though *self-study* and *self-knowledge*. There is nothing mysterious about it, as in black or white magic, nor, as is popularly imagined, does its scope and significance lie in the swallowing of crushed glass or cyanide, lying on beds of nails, or walking on hot coals. Hatha Yoga is only a form of "personal hygiene" which maintains perfect health in a human being through physical, mental, moral and spiritual training. The Yoga system which has been practiced in India since at least the time of the Epics, that is, 1000 B.C. (the excavations in the Indus Valley show the science was known in 3000 B.C.), supersedes modern knowledge of hygiene in many ways. It affords to men longevity, resistence to disease, the growth of a beautiful body, and mental and spiritual sublimation.

2. CHRISTIANITY AND YOGA

I have said that the sincere practitioner of any of the world's religions may be called a yogi. In fact the *true* Christian way of life *is* YOGA. Mahatma Gandhi, the saviour of modern India, who was well versed in the principles of yoga read the Bible daily and taught from it. His greatest weapon against foreign domination and oppression was the first *yama* of yoga, the first of the five prescribed Restraints, which Patanjali and other ancient yogis said must be practiced faithfully, before setting out on the journey of yoga. It was non-violence, or *ahimsa,* as it is known in Sanscrit, a word which Gandhi made world famous. How remarkably like Christ's teachings this is! This great master taught "Whosoever shall smite thee on thy right cheek, turn to him the other also."[3]

Even the list of Restraints *(yama-s)* given by Patanjali may have come straight out of the Bible: "The Restraints are non-violence, truth, non-stealing, chastity and non-possession."

Vivekananda (founder of the Ramakrishna-Vivekananda Mission in America) quoted from the Bible in his books and lectures and urged on people the teachings of Christ. And his teacher Ramakrishna wrote: "Through Yoga a Hindu becomes a better Hindu, a Christian a better Christian, a Mohammedan a better Mohammedan, and a Jew a better Jew!" Yoga does not conflict with Christian teachings. It can be of great use to the West in spite of the dissenting and mistaken opinion that yoga is a religious revelation which is only applicable to the East. As Selvarajan Yesudian says in his *"Yoga Uniting East and West"* (Harper and Brothers, New York), "In the Bible Jesus teaches us two paths: the path of the SELF: 'I am the way, the truth and the life.'[4] This is the inner, individual way — Yoga — the way of the Orient. **And the** second: 'Thou shalt love thy neighbor as thyself.'[5] This is the outward, community path — the way of the Occident. Our life becomes perfect only when we fulfill both of these teachings of

---

[3] The Bible, Luke 6:29
[4] The Bible, John 14·6
[5] The Bible, Leviticus 19 18.

Christ. Each of the two paths includes the other, but only when we reach the *end of the path we are following*. The one path achieves unity from outside inward, the other from within outward. If we follow both paths, we reach perfection — the point where the paths meet — much more quickly."

3. THE PHILOSOPHY OF YOGA

This is chiefly meant to be a handbook for the practice of the postures, breathing exercises and meditation of Hatha Yoga for the acquiring of radiant health and tranquillity in both body and mind. However, a short outline of the philosophy and forms of yoga will not be out of place. Those students who are more interested in the practical part of this book, the exercises, may reserve this chapter and the next for a later reading when they have mastered a few of them. They will have then begun to *feel* within themselves intuitively, so to speak, the ultimate purpose of all forms of yoga, and that of Hatha Yoga in particular. The student should, however, remember that Hatha Yoga contains within itself some of the basic elements of all the other forms of yoga which will be described in this chapter.

The philosophy of yoga starts with the conception that any idea which is not confirmed by experience must remain mere speculation. Our knowledge is therefore circumscribed by the limited nature of our mental and physical experiences. Western science may have extended sensory perception through the invention of microscopes, seismographs, Geiger-counters or the firing of atoms of electrified hydrogen into a tremendous magnetic field when a "universe in miniature," an exact copy of the universe, is formed in a test tube. However, Hindu philosophers say that sensory knowledge, this "outward knowing," is limited to appearances. And Appearance is *Māyā* or Illusion. The inner reality of the world of appearance presents itself to us obscured by many changing forms. Our intellectual knowledge is also finite, a mere crumb of the truth, since it is limited by form. So the Hindus have declared that "outward knowing" is "partly knowing." It is not the total *experience,* the *full knowledge,* one may have of anything. So they say that the only way to know anything, say an apple, both inwardly and outwardly, is to identify ourselves with it, *be* one with it. Then we experience and know the apple *fully,* and its relation to us and the universe. We are one with the apple and have true knowledge of it. We have identified ourselves with the apple and we know more about it than when we regarded it solely from the external point of view — or from the viewpoint of "outward knowing."

That is the meaning of the Sanscrit word *yoga* which derives from the same root as the English word "yoke" — identification of ourselves with an object or cosmos or SELF through "union." Identification, "union," yoking or yoga with divinity is called "self-realization." This was also the way of the Christian saints such as St. John of the Cross or St. Theresa of Avila.

That is the purpose of yoga: — to transcend, as did the saints, the limits of the "gross" physical self and achieve *self-realization* through releasing the subtle self.

We have heard of "subtle" beings such as Angels who know all things. It is the philosophy of yoga that we can transcend the limits of our Consciousness and perceive all things of which our senses afford only the merest hints or glimpses. The cultivation of supra-sensory perception is one of the aims of yoga. Exercising parts of the body which normally do not get any exercise is one of the purposes of Hatha Yoga. In this form of Yoga special exercises have been devised to aid the process. That is why this form of the science is the most useful for the preservation of mental and bodily health.

In general, however, the purpose of yoga is the knowing of SELF. But there exist several methods of "knowing." According to the method we choose we may arrive at different contradictory conclusions. They are all nevertheless facets of the same Supreme Reality, and together make up TRUTH.

These are the six different methods of "knowing":

SĀNKHYA or Cosmological method which operates through intellectual knowledge.

VAISHESHIKA or Naturalistic method which operates through sensorial experiences.

NYĀYA or logical method which operates through dialectics.

YOGA or the method Identification and Union which operates through supra-sensory perception and control of the body, the senses, and the inner faculties.

20

MIMĀNSA or the method of Rituals which operates through the Revealed Scriptures.

VEDĀNTA or the method of metaphysics which operates through metaphysical speculation.

Our ancients say that of all these Vedānta and Yoga are the best. Vedānta is the philosophy which was taught by Swami Vivekananda in America and which has today won the allegiance of several writers in California like Aldous Huxley, Gerald Heard and Christopher Isherwood. Vedānta shows us the final objective of our "knowing," while Yoga shows us the way to directly experience what is worth "knowing."

There are innumerable forms of yoga. This is inevitable since the whole of cosmos is the Supreme Truth and any part or aspect of it may be used as the means to reach it. This is a fundamental concept of yoga.

In Hatha Yoga, for instance, the body and its health is the chosen object, and the practitioner is enjoined to meditate on any one part of his body like the tip of his nose or the centre of the forehead, on an external object like a photograph or the tip of a candle flame. Through this particularized approach he may become more intensely aware of the workings of his body and achieve extraordinary power over them.

4. THE FORMS OF YOGA

Though there are innumerable approaches to the Supreme Spirit, or if you will, the Supreme Truth (all forms of knowledge are finally a form of yoga) and, therefore, innumerable forms of yoga are possible, there are nine chief forms which are commonly practiced in India.

The first is HATHA YOGA, which is the most popular. According to the verses in *Goraksha Samhitā* and *Hatha Yoga Pradipikā*: "The syllable 'Ha' represents the sun, and the syllable 'tha' represents the moon, and hence the yoking together *(yoga)* of the sun and moon is *Hatha Yoga.*"

This polarity which on our terrestrial globe is symbolized by the warm aspect of the sun and the cold aspect of the moon is present throughout the universe. Within our bodies these positive and negative aspects are represented in our subtle and gross bodies. In our subtle body they appear as two currents (in our spine) along which our perceptions travel between the subtle plexus at the base of the spinal column (*Mulādhāra Chakra,* or four leaved lotus) and the subtle plexus at the top of the brain (*Sahasrāra,* or lotus of a thousand petals). These are indicated in Figure I. The negative current travels along the left channel called *Idā* and the positive along the right channel called *Pingalā.* (Figure I). In our gross bodies as our ancients have said the negative and positive aspects are represented by respiration which cools and digestion which warms up the body. It is by achieving a perfect equilibrium between these negative and positive influences in the body that the Hatha yogi reaches his goal. This equilibrium is symbolized in the religions of the world by the six-pointed star made by the super-imposition of two triangles. It represents the man who has attained Yoga or Union — or Man-God.

By the attainment of equilibrium the Hatha Yogi is able to concentrate on any particular part of his body and direct his whole attention to it. For instance, he could force his whole attention towards his lungs until he becomes solely aware of the single thought "I am my lungs." In a similar way he becomes conscious of every nerve cen-

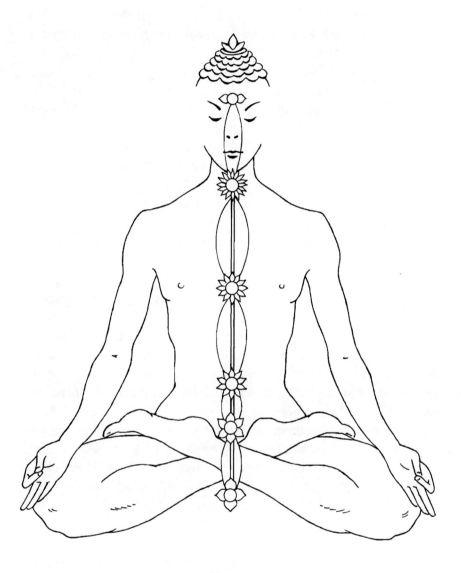

Figure 1   Positive and Negative Currents of the Subtle Body
Which Travel within the Spinal Column

23

tre in his body, and of the two life currents which animate him. By their exercise and perfect control through Hatha Yoga he achieves vitality and health.

His consciousness may now be expanded until he is aware that everything that exists in the universe has this polarity and rhythm which is LIFE! That is why the Hindus say symbolically that everything on the earth and the universe, including the flowers, stones, heavenly bodies and ourselves are manifestations of Natarajah, or Shiva as Lord of the Dance. Without the dance's pulse the world would end.

Natarajah has also been constantly designated by the Hindus as the Lord of Creation and Destruction which is constantly going on in the Universe.

The constant creation and destruction of matter is a fundamental tenet of Indian philosophy and science.

I have already remarked that just as the Earth has two poles, so have our bodies. The negative is the plexus at the base of the spine and the positive the plexus at the top of the brain. Between these two, and carried by the spine, is a current of extremely high frequency, which is LIFE.

This principle of life permeates the entire universe. Whenever the creative principle abandons its Pristine Form and splits in two, the opposing polarities are born, the negative and positive. Between the two pulsing and rhythm begins and thus life is born. Life manifests itself only according to necessity. In the case of man he grew his brain on top of the spinal column since there was the necessity to feel and think. He grew the other organs of his body so he may smell, see, hear, taste and perpetuate himself through reproduction. He developed his nerves to contain the electrical currents which constitute life.

Life within himself is what man refers to as "I." This "I," this SELF, is only the Pristine Form which has always existed! So the SELF which was never born and can never die has always existed and is indestructible. Our life is immortal. It is only our gross body, the outward manifestation of self on the material plane, which dies.

When life, conscious of itself, presents this idea through his mind to man, he reaches self-realization, or consciousness of self. Then the self, carried in the body, radiates LIFE through the entire body, via the nervous system, and the body is filled with equilibrium.

Man, who through his own volition gradually assumed his material shape, growing his sense organs and his brain to experience himself is indeed "the first matter which has begun to contemplate itself." And the Hatha Yogis believe that through proper relaxing postures, systems of breathing and proper meditation they should be able to experience the Primary Force, which divided into two opposed polarities, and creating a life current between the two, gradually evolved into man.

Not only that, they believe in further evolution. Just as Man grew the most perfect brain of all living things on top of the spinal cord in response to his needs, they know that any other part of the nervous system may be developed into a "brain." We know that when an important nerve of the body is destroyed, another nerve will often take on its functions. The yogi understands this principle and extends it. He directs his attention to various parts of his nervous system and through years of concentration develops them as if they were "supplementary brains" so that his organism becomes the most fully conscious of any.

There are nine chief forms of yoga:

1. HATHA YOGA: or self-realization through health and strength.
2. RĀJA YOGA: or The Royal Way of self-realization.
3. JNANA YOGA: or The Way of Wisdom for self-realization.
4. KRIYA YOGA: or the system of self-realization through prānāyāma and concentration.
5. MANTRA YOGA: or The Yoga of Hermetic Utterances.
6. YANTRA YOGA: or the Yoga of Mystical Diagrams Representing the Principal Forms.
7. LAYA YOGA: or the Yoga of Mergence.
8. KUNDALINI YOGA: or the Yoga of Awakening the Mysterious Power (Kundalini).
9. BHAKTI YOGA: or the Yoga of self-realization through Love.

Through Hatha Yoga the body will be kept more fit than is possible through any other known system of physical culture. Not only are the limbs exercised and proper breathing taught, but the seemingly impossible task of massaging the internal glands is achieved. The ultimate goal is the perfect control of the whole organism. This, of course, need not concern my present readers, since only Hatha Yogis who wish to proceed further in the science make such control an end in itself. Hatha Yoga is really the preparation of mind and body, through health and vitality, for a higher form of Yoga, Rāja Yoga, which is the reason it has been called "the ladder to Rāja Yoga": "The science of Hatha Yoga is the ladder up which those climb who wish to reach the higher regions of the Royal Path." — *Goraksha Samhitā.*

The second form of yoga is RĀJA YOGA, or the Kingly Form of Yoga. The *Hatha Yoga Pradipikā* tells us that it is only for the sake of knowing Rāja Yoga that Hatha Yoga is taught. It is the peak of the yoga system, all the other forms being merely preparatory.

The Kingly Form of Yoga contains something of all the other methods and a great deal more. It teaches us that we are all slaves of the movements of the mind, of our fleeting moods and emotions, and that the intellect is the agent of our freedom. When the agitation of the mind is stilled we acquire supra-sensory perceptions and perceive the unity of all things. Stilling his senses the Rāja Yogi has perfect control of his inner and outer faculties and learns the distinction between Self and non-Self, which reveals itself to him as the pure form of Nature *(Prakriti).* Withdrawn from all worldly associations he reaches *Samādhi* (the Bible's "the peace that passeth all understanding") and he becomes absorbed into the Infinite.

In this state past and future and finite become merged into one. The body becomes immune to heat, cold and disease. It subsists for days on end without air, water or food. The liberated mind, freed from the body, roams the Universe at will and no knowledge is beyond it. Through the exercise of Rāja Yoga many yogis have gained knowledge of the spheres (bhuvana jnāna) and knowledge of the stars *(tārā-vyuha-jnāna).*

The other forms of knowledge this yoga confers are called Supreme Sight *(siddha darshana),* freedom from hunger and thirst *(kshut-pipasa-nivritti)* and knowledge of the various parts of the body *(kāyā-vyuha-jnāna).*

The third form of yoga is JNĀNA YOGA, or Yoga of the Intellect.

26

It is the yoga of the scientist. Through perfect discrimination and self-analysis one realizes that the Primal Force is distinct from all forms, and one merges with it.

The fourth yoga is KRIYA YOGA. It is a system through which *kundalini* (dormant power) in the practitioner is raised to cosmic consciousness by certain techniques which consist of breathing, meditation and concentration, coordinated at one and the same time. It should be learnt under a *guru* (teacher). It teaches us to look for traits in others which we think we possess, instead of criticizing others for their faults.

MANTRA YOGA is based on the fact that the rhythmic repetition of sound has physical effects. For instance a glass could be shattered by sound if its frequency equals that of the glass. Soldiers marching across a bridge are ordered to break step since bridges have often collapsed when the natural frequency of the bridge was the same as the beat of the marching.

In this yoga the mind and body are trained by yoga breathing and repetition of words and sentences chosen for their vibratory effect. It should appeal specially to poets, orators and singers. This Yoga teaches us that words of anger or words that are ugly are detrimental to the human organism (through their inimical vibrations) while words of happiness or love are beneficial. On the philosophical plane it teaches that just as ether is more real than the temporarily polarized ether which constitutes all visible things, there is a greater reality to be grasped behind the names and forms which describe the manifest world to us.

In a similar way YANTRA YOGA makes use of mystic diagrams which represent the principal forms *(yantra-s)*, while LAYA YOGA entails all the exercises of Hatha Yoga together with abstinences, self-withdrawal and deep concentration. In this yoga special attention is paid to "hearing of inner sound" *(Nāda-anusandhāna-vidhi)*. The *Rik Veda* (1500-500 B.C.) describes the process in beautiful words in the *Nāda-bindu-Upanishad (31-41)*: "Seated in the Posture of Attainment and keeping the gesture of the Pervander (i.e. keeping the eyes wide open without twinkling) the yogi should constantly listen to the inner sound with his right ear. This sound when constantly practiced will cover all the outer sounds. (The Yogi) with the help of that which is his own, conquers all that is external to him, and reaches the fourth (unmanifest) state. At first many great sounds are heard, but, with practice, more and more subtle sounds are perceived. At first the sounds are like those produced by the ocean, or by a cloud, a drum, a waterfall; then like the sounds of a small drum, that of a bell, or of a musical instrument; finally it becomes like the tinkling of bells, a flute, a lute, or a bee."

"Thus are the many sounds heard growing subtler and subtler. Even when the louder sounds, like that of the big drum, are heard, the yogi should keep listening to the subtler ones. The mind should not be allowed to abandon the grosser ones for the subtler ones or the subtler for the grosser ones, even if it finds it pleasant. It should stick to the sound which pleased it first and dissolve with it. The mind lost in that sound forgets everything outward, and merges itself into the sound, as milk mixes with water, finally to dissolve with it in the ether of consciousness. Controlling his mind, the yogi, by constant practice, becomes indifferent to everything else and is attracted by such sounds as transport him beyond the mind. Leaving all thoughts and all efforts, meditating on sound alone his mind merges into sound."[6]

The inner sound is heard when the mind has been stilled and the vital breath brought into the sixth centre; but soon comes liberation from the inner sound itself when the yogi merges into *Shabda* (The Principle of Word) which is what the Bible means when it says "In the beginning was the Word, and the Word was with God, and the Word was God. The same was in the beginning with God. All things were made by him; . . . and the life was the light of men." (John: I 1-4) The "Word" of the Bible and the Principle of Word *(shabda)* are one and the same thing.

These sounds raise the hair on the head and it grows giddy. The mouth salivates. But the initiated one follows the path he has chosen with steadfastness. Just like the bee intoxicated with the honey cares no longer for the fragrance which first attracted it, even so the expert soon forgets the inner sounds enveloping him and passes into the

---

[6] *Yoga The Method of Re-Integration* by Alain Danielou, University Books, New York.

28

Principle of Word and is one with it. Then in his heart he hears an all-pervasive sound he has never heard before.

It is in Laya Yoga that the coiled and dormant nervous energy *(kundalini)* which lies between the anus and the generative organs, where it is coiled three and a half times like a serpent (see Figure 1) is awakened and made to rise through the six plexuses in the spine to the lotus-of-a-thousand-petals, the plexus on top of the brain. Yoga says there are eleven pairs of cranial nerves and the longest of them, the right vagus, connects the brain with the solar plexus below which the *kundalini chakra* or the serpent power lies coiled. In the poetic languages of our ancient books the purpose of this yoga is to awake this serpent power and catch its tail as it rises.

It is in the solar plexus that we most feel tension, excitement, fear and love, and it is this region that is most affected when we violently retch due to any poisonous substance in the body, or any mental state. I have seen a man retch when he was told a disgusting story. That violent retching has sometimes cured the insane, conclusively proves the intimate connection that exists between the *kundalini chakra* and the brain.

Exercise of the *kundalini* through this yoga brings peace of mind and serenity. It is also taught apart from Laya Yoga in a system called Kundalini Yoga.

The ninth form of yoga is BHAKTI YOGA or the Yoga of Devotion, and it is said to be part of Mantra Yoga. It has a strong emotional coloring and achieves self-realization through the pursuit of devotion and worship.

I have not enumerated the different forms of yoga here to confuse the reader, but to give an indication of the Science's scope. Actually, the reader will find this book (which I have based on my experience and experiments at the Yoga Health Sanatorium) easy to follow. The eight different steps in Yoga which take one gradually stage by stage to the highest self-awareness have been simplified in this book. These eight steps are:

1. YAMA: Eradication of mental and physical ailments to create bodily and mental peace.
2. NIYAMA: The cultivation of virtue.

3. ĀSANA: Yoga posture.
4. PRĀNĀYĀMA: Yoga breathing.
5. PRATYĀHARĀ: Control of senses.
6. DHĀRANA: Concentration.
7. DHYĀNA: Meditation.
8. SAMĀDHI: The state of bliss.

These have been simplified here to such an extent that they can be practiced to achieve maximum benefit, in the shortest possible time, while carrying on one's usual run of duties in the western world.

5. YOGA TRANSCENDS THE PRINCIPLE OF RELATIVITY AND DUALITY

Yoga teaches that the physical universe is conditioned by *Maya,* the law of relativity and duality. *Maya* or Illusion is the World of Appearance which veils the true reality. We only know it from its outward form and that is constantly changing.

Newton's law of motion is a mayic concept. He said that "To every action there is always an equal and contrary reaction; the mutual actions of any two bodies are always equal and oppositely directed." He added that the existence of a single force is impossible. There must always be the polarity which is characteristic of the universe and man. Force can only exist in equal and opposite pairs. For instance the earth has a positive and negative pole, as has the atom its protons and electrons. Similarly, electricity is the force derived from the attraction and repulsion of negative and positive particles. This relativity and duality, *Maya,* permeates all creation and it is the express method of the yogi to transcend it, and experience the Supreme Truth, THE PRIMAL FORCE.

It is after good mental and physical health has been attained through *yama, niyama* and *āsana* that the higher stages of yoga can be attempted and this will be, at present, difficult to achieve for the majority of people. The *yamas,* or virtues, to be cultivated by a student of yoga consist of *ahimsa* or non-injury, truthfulness, chastity in thought and deed, non-covetousness and selfless service. The *niyamas* include the study of yoga, Vedas, scriptures, the Bible and eastern philosophy as well as contentment, internal and external cleanliness, belief in cosmic supremacy, fasting, repetition of *mantras* both verbally and mentally, and pilgrimage. The demands of *yama* and *niyama* (Restraints and Observances) are difficult to fulfill in the Western world. However, the Western student should realize that the method described in this book can lead to benefits other than merely mental and physical well-

31

being, but that these should be taught to him by a teacher *(guru)* and not through the written word!

The yogi knows that there is no material universe. It is all illusion. Therefore, in the highest forms of yoga (like Rāja Yoga) he transcends it in *samādhi* when he becomes part of the Primal Force, or Light, and he reaches illumination. However, it must be made clear that the exercises in this book are designed merely to relax and strengthen the mind and body, and to release the vital energies in the spine for the organism's proper functioning and well-being.

6. EFFECT OF YOGA ON

THE ENDOCRINE GLANDS

The ductless glands which are so called because they pour their secretions not into ducts but directly into the blood stream are among the most important organs in the body. They are the chemical factories which manufacture the hormones which affect every function of the body, physiologically and psychologically. They control our growth, structure, height, weight and personality. They determine our physical and mental activity, and our lifespan. They are supreme arbiters in determining the shapes of our faces, our complexion, our personality and the characteristic difference between male and female.

The manufacture and the distribution of these hormones can be greatly affected by the mental state of the individual concerned. For example, when we are frightened the currents along our nerves are affected, which in turn affect the composition of the blood. The adrenal or the suprarenal capsules are then activated and pour their various hormones into the blood stream, quickening the heart beats, raising the blood pressure and injecting sugar to provide the extra energy that is called for. Yoga teaches that the mental state has tremendous physical effects.

The chief endocrine glands in the body are the adrenal or suprarenal capsules, which are situated above the kidneys; the pineal and pituitary which are respectively in the brain and at the base of the brain; the thyroid and parathyroid, in the neck; the coccygeal, in front of the tip of the coccyx, the last vertebra; the thymus, in the chest; the carotid, between the fork of the carotid artery in the neck; the gonads or sex glands, pancreas, liver and spleen. (Figure 2, p. 34). In the yoga system of psychophysiological hygiene all these glands are exercised.

The adrenals weigh about a sixth of an ounce each and secrete, among others, two important hormones — adrenalin and cortin. When we are frightened or angry they pour adrenalin into the blood increasing our pulse and blood pressure and giving us more energy through the

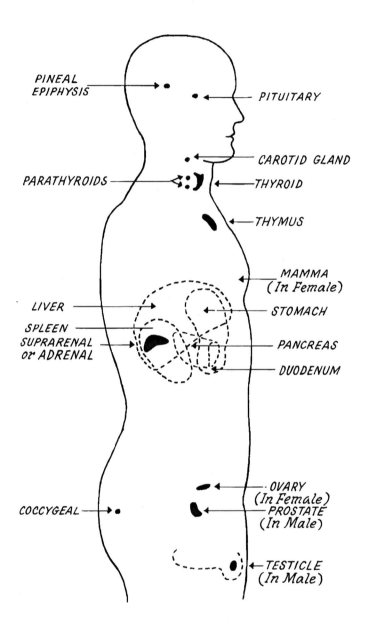

PINEAL
EPIPHYSIS

PITUITARY

CAROTID GLAND

PARATHYROIDS

THYROID

THYMUS

MAMMA
(In Female)

LIVER

STOMACH

SPLEEN

SUPRARENAL
or ADRENAL

PANCREAS

DUODENUM

OVARY
(In Female)

COCCYGEAL

PROSTATE
(In Male)

TESTICLE
(In Male)

Figure 2   The Ductless Glands and Other Important Organs

34

injection of extra sugar. It also stops bleeding by contracting the arteries. These two hormones also influence sexual characteristics. Overactivity of the adrenal cortex, for instance, results in masculine traits in women.

Deficiency in the adrenal hormones brings on low blood pressure, a lack of muscular tone and loss of strength. It also lowers the immunity of the organism to germs. The yoga exercises which are most beneficial to the adrenal glands are the Hare Posture and Posterior-Stretching Posture (*Paschimatanāsana,* p. 86).

The pineal gland, about a third of an inch long and weighing about two grains is situated in the brain and was known to the ancients as 'the third eye.' Representations of the god Shiva show this eye in the middle of the forehead. The yogis say that it plays a great part in thought transference. They also believe that through the concentration of the vital energies of the body on it (and its development) it both transmits and receives telepathic messages.

The pituitary gland located at the base of the brain reacts to strong emotions. The pituitary hormone is more responsible than any other for our personalities. Too much of it and a man becomes ruthless and violent; too little, and he becomes a weakling. The right amount and a man has initiative and courage. An excess of the secretion will produce a giant and too little a dwarf. The pituitary affects skeletal growth, sex development, carbohydrate metabolism, water metabolism, and the functions of the circulatory and respiratory systems. When it functions defectively the thyroid takes on some of the work since there is a balancing action between the two. Among yoga exercises, all those of the 'inverted' type like the Head Stand *(Sirshāsana)* send a huge supply of new blood to the pituitary and are beneficial for it.

The shield-shaped thyroid which is situated on each side of the Adam's apple was known to the Greeks though they did not know its functions (*thureoeides* in Greek means shield-shaped). Scientists have shown that it is much affected by acute mental depression and its condition is one of the causes of myxoedemia. Too much thyroxin results in opthalmic goiter and too little in loss of weight and of reserves of calcium and fat. It also leads to lowering of body temperatures and breathing rate, depressed activity and underdeveloped and function-

35

ally deficient sex glands. *Sharvangāsana* or the Shoulder Stand and *Matysyāsana* or the Fish Posture are some of the most wonderful Yoga exercises to keep the thyroid in good health.

The parathyroids in the neck (Figure 2, p. 34) have a great deal to do with the health of the nervous system, and the calcium content of the blood which in turn controls bone growth. Deficiency of the parathyroid hormone causes the organic calcium in the body to be eliminated without being used.

Calcium helps in the clotting of blood. I know many people who could bleed to death on the slightest injury because their blood cannot clot. I myself have been noting the effect of the parathyroids on my own body for the last ten years. I am regular in my exercises of the Shoulder Stand and the Fish Posture which keep the parathyroids and thyroids in condition. But the day I miss them, which seldom happens, I feel I have been lacking something throughout the day. With these exercises the clotting quality of my blood has been steadily improving.

Little is known about the function of the coccygeal glands which are a small cluster of cells in front of the tip of the last vertebra. However the Yogis believe that they are a centre of vitality in the body and that they can be exercised and awakened for the benefit of the whole organism through yogic breathing in *Padmāsana* or the Lotus Posture. *Salabāsana* or the Locust Posture also tones up the coccygeal — as well as the liver and pancreas.

The generative glands or the gonads are responsible for an individual remaining in an optimum state of health, as well as for his or her sexuality. They maintain youthful vigor, prevent the onset of senility, and exercise a deep psychological and physiological influence on the organism. They are responsible for the development of specific male and female characteristics. The exercise for toning up the gonads is *Padmāsana* or Lotus Seat.

7. *AYURVEDA:* THE PSYCHOSOMATIC MEDICAL SYSTEM OF THE INDIANS

Dr. Henry R. Zimmer in his two published lectures at Johns Hopkins University (*Hindu Medicine* by Henry R. Zimmer, The Johns Hopkins Press, Baltimore) gave a very concise and admirable description of the Indian concept of the human body, at the very start of his second lecture: "The Hindu concept of the human body, throughout the history of Indian thought, is characterized by the belief that the body is a manifestation of divine substance and energy, as is the whole universe. The principal forces and faculties which abide in the organism, giving it life and supporting its processes, are microcosmic counterparts of the powers which pervade the cosmic body and maintain it through their various antagonistic and co-operative activities. The Hindu devotee who practices Tantric ritual is taught to think of himself not as the ordinary being whose duties he performs and whose role he plays in the course of his daily routine, but as a microcosmic sum total of the divine cosmic forces. This he realizes by withdrawing into . . . meditation . . . . He cultivates an awareness of the ever-present assembly of divine energies within the frame of his mortal existence, awakening them from the dormant state of unconsciousness through a ritual of gestures and invocations." It is thus seen that the Indian thinks of the microcosm of the body as part of the macrocosm of Primal Force and that his approach to it and its diseases is therefore bound to be somewhat different from the customary Western approach.

According to Ayurveda, the Indian "Science of Life," diseases are not physiological alone, but psychological as well. Ayurveda is therefore a psychosomatic medical system. "Physiological and psychological actions in the human system are so inextricably interwoven that to the Hindu specialist physiology divorced from psychology would be too

37

crude to deserve the name of science," wrote Dr. S. M. Mitra who in 1905 was the first Hindu doctor to practice the ayurvedic system of medicine in the West.

Ayurveda, The Science of Life, does not directly treat the simple microscopically and chemically demonstrable part of a disease, but its more subtle and root causes. For instance we know it is the mind that hears and sees and that ears and eyes are merely the outward organs through which the brain records these sensations. As Dr. Mitra says, "The Hindu physician does not believe in fighting disease with disease, poison with poison, or germs with germs. His idea of healing is elimination, not suppression."

Ayurvedic physicians believe in transforming Nature from a moderately good healer to a powerful healer. They know that most common diseases are due to depletion of nerve-force. So if the brain cells are worn out, for instance, they do not attempt to restore vitality to them but awaken thousands of hitherto unused cells in the body and make them take on the functions of the exhausted cells.

Yoga improves the production of nerve-force by bringing a more liberal supply of fresh blood to the nerves and by automatic massage through stretching or the rapid vibrations of tissues. In *Shirshāsana,* a greater supply of blood is sent to the brain since we are standing on our heads. In *Sarvangāsana,* since we are standing on our necks and shoulders, the thyroid gets a more liberal flow. Increased blood flow to various parts of the body is also accomplished by putting checks at different places. In *Sarvangāsana* the carotids are checked by the chin lock.

Ayurveda and yoga have still much to give to the West. The western system was originally brought to the West by the Arabs who came into touch with India in the Seventh Century. Many Hindu medical treatises were translated into Arabic. The first alchemists of Europe (who were the first chemists) were Arabs, and European medicine up to the 17th Century was practically based on the Indian. The name of India's most famous physician, Charaka of the 4th Century B.C., occurs repeatedly in Latin translations from the Arabic of Avicenna, Serapion and Rhazes. It is interesting to note that many of the Western names for parts of the body are derived from Sanscrit:

38

SANSCRIT	EUROPEAN
Shirobram	Cerebrum
Shirobiloma	Cerebellum

And in *Shiva Samhitā**we learn the ancients even knew that the central nervous system is composed of grey and white matters. Since the humoral theory of the Indians is similar to that of Hippocrates, Europeans have said that the Indians borrowed it from the Greeks. But how may this be when the humoral theory is mentioned in the *Rigveda*, many, many centuries before Hippocrates?

In spite of this tendency, we are today becoming more aware that the East has much yet to give — including medical theory. For instance, Indians have long studied cancer and they have claimed that the cure lies in prevention by abstaining from pork and underdone meat (a daily intake of pineapple juice and honey and some food flavoured with cardomom is also recommended).

---

*Tr by Rai Bahadur S C. Vidyarnava (Panini Office, Allahabad).

8. YOGA AND LONGEVITY

Yoga exercises draw huge quantities of blood to the spine. All the nerves which emanate from the spine are consequently toned up. The forward and backward bending exercises, and the lateral ones, not only send up blood to the brain but exercise many other organs of the body. They render elastic and supple the spinal cord and its branchings, as well as the muscular tissues. In Europe we have often heard that a man is as old as his arteries, but a yogi would rather say that a man is merely as old as his tissues.

Beyond the gross idea of tissues he also has the subtle one of the nerve-force which travels along the *nādi-s* (astral tubes) and charges the whole battery of the body. The state of flux of the nerve-force also determines age.

The Indians knew as far back as the *Rig-Veda* (1,500 B.C.) that heat, light, and the bio-thermal or bio-combustion organization in the body *(pitta)* and nerve-force or electricity *(prānā)* are all related terms. For instance Charaka says: "The life-span, complexion, vitality, good health, enthusiasm, plumpness, glow, vital essence, lustre, heat and electricity *(prānā)* are derived from the thermogenetic process in the body." Some of the other verses of the *Charaka Samhitā* are also interesting (translated by P. M. Mehta in *Anemia and Ayurveda, The Journal of Indian Medical Sciences,* September 1952): "It is fire alone that, located in bio-combustion, gives rise to good and evil consequences according as it is in a normal or an abnormal condition. These consequences are, digestion and indigestion, vision and loss of vision, normality and abnormality of temperature, the healthy and diseased complexion, intrepidity and fear, anger and delight, confusion and lucidity and such other pairs of opposites. Then the five kinds of latent heat innate in each of the proto-elements of the body, earth, water (the organization of fluid balance in the body), wind (organization of vital balance in the body through breath) and ether (electricity and light), digest each its own corresponding component proto-element in the ingested food which is a compound of the proto-elements. Just as a quality in the substances nourishes individually its corresponding

40

quality in the body, as for example the proto-element of earth in the body is nourished by the proto-element of earth in the article ingested, similarly the other proto-elements nourish their corresponding qualities thus making for complete nourishment. The body-sustaining elements, which are seven, undergo combustion by their innate heat and each of them gets transformed into two products namely excretory and vital substances. Thus has been described the metabolic function of the thermal element in the five proto-elements. The gastric fire is considered the supreme king of all the metabolic agents in the body. They are all originated from it. Their waxing and waning are dependent upon the increase and decrease of the gastric fire. Therefore one should strive to preserve the gastric fire with the fuel of wholesome food and drink taken in the right manner. For in the proper maintenance of the gastric fire are based long life and vitality." These verses from Charaka make it clear that Indians had a clear idea of the relationship between heat, electricity and light and the human body.

The yoga exercises which tone up the nerve-force or electric flux in the spine preserve its flexibility. A man is never old, if his spine is flexible. In spite of his many years he will be young in spirit — like a young man of twenty. On the other hand, a man of twenty would feel and look like a man of eighty if his spine were not flexible. I have observed without exception, that to practice the exercises for even ten minutes daily helps to improve the flexibility of the spine.

Everyone wants to enjoy eternal youth. How to attain it has been for generations the problem of scientists and philosophers the world over. Today all of us can practice yoga which not only teaches how to overcome old age, but also, how to grow younger!

Yoga teaches how to keep the glands throughout the body in good health, and avoid the physical and psychological difficulties which arise when they are not functioning properly. One of the causes of old age, as we know, is that the conjunctive cells replace those in the bodily tissues, causing physical atrophy and the hardening of arteries, or replace the cells of the brain itself, impairing its functions, like memory, the preservation of physical equilibrium, and the control of the movements of the limbs. Arteriosclerosis is the evil genius in a great many deaths.

Another major factor in ageing and death is that the interstitial glands are impaired. They are the chief dynamos in the body for brain power, vitality and youthfulness. If a man is deprived of these glands he will suddenly grow old as if a magician's curse had struck him. The practice of yoga, which involves no extra expenditure, keeps the interstitial glands in perfect order until the *mahāsamādhi* itself, or the yogi's final conscious exit from the body.

Yoga also rejuvenates the body through *Prānāyāma* or the breathing exercises. All yogis are taught to inhale and exhale slowly and smoothly. It is a fact that we breathe very fast when we are disturbed by anger or fear (which, as we have seen in a previous chapter, is detrimental to the blood stream and the whole body). When we are concentrating on doing something, like reading, we breathe more slowly. In sleep too, when breathing is unconscious, and is measured and smooth, we are rejuvenating our body and mind. Slow and rhythmic breathing has a very beneficial effect, and, when properly done, tends to prolong life.

In yogic *samādhi* the outgoing breath is not wasted but is made to activate more nervous energy (electricity) which flushes the entire system and rejuvenates it. More will be said on this point in the chapter on Yoga breathing *(prānāyāma)*. It affects all the cells of the human body. Yoga breathing not only oxygenates and decarbonizes the blood but in *samādhi* (meditation), unlike in sleep, it *consciously* releases the healing nerve-force through the entire body via the power houses of the brain and the six plexuses of the spine (coccygeal, sacral, lumbar, dorsal, cervical and medullary). The healing force is electricity *(prāna)*, according to yoga, and it travels through the astral tubes *(nadi-s)*.

The stopping of the outgoing breath to preserve the nerve-energy in the body is described in the *Bhagavad Gita* (IV, 29): "Yet some offer . . . . . the out-going into the in-coming breath, and the in-coming into the out-going, stopping the courses of the in-coming and outgoing breath, constantly practicing the regulation of the vital energy."[7] If this sounds somewhat quaintly put it must be remembered that it is

---

[7] *Srimad-Bhagavad-Gita* tr. by Swami Swarupananda, Advaita Ashrama, Himalayas.

not a translation of Sanscrit prose but of classical Sanscrit poetry composed before 1,000 B.C.

Besides the control of breath there are many other yoga exercises which help in revitalization and rejuvenation. To take the Head Stand, for instance, it corrects a fault of nature. Man's brain, because of his upright posture, may have at times an inadequate supply of blood. Since modern experiments have shown that an increase in blood supply to the brain results in greater mental alertness and activity it stands to reason that to keep our minds young and healthy we must practice the Head Stand.

The different yoga exercises described in this book have, similarly, various parts to play in keeping the organism's vitality and youthfulness. These will be described in the appropriate sections.

The yogis also have a rejuvenating treatment called *"kayakalpa."* It means "a new life through a change of body." This is a science in itself and is so arduous with fasting and a special diet (this was in a sense Mahatma Gandhi's method) that I shall not attempt to describe it. But what is contained in this book, if faithfully practiced, should enable us all to live to a hundred.

Part Two

9. YOGA POSTURES, OR

ĀSANA-S

In the Western world cancer, heart disease and mental disorders are among the most numerous causes of death. I am convinced that most of them could be prevented or delayed through the practice of yoga. On account of improper breathing and faulty oxygenation, the blood becomes chemically unbalanced. Toxic substances are not eliminated and the endocrine glands cease to function adequately. In a highly toxic state the body is now prone to disease and death. The practice of yoga would relieve such a condition:

1. Through elimination of impurities by restoring normal respirtion, perspiration, digestion, assimilation, urination and excretion.
2. By resting different parts of the body, including the heart and mind, both unconsciously and consciously.
3. By rejuvenating the particular organs where degeneration has set in through transmission of more *prāna* (cosmic energy) to them.
4. By reducing expenditure of energy through the relaxation of mind and body.
5. By proper diet as more fully discussed in Chapter 16.

The first steps in yoga, besides yama and niyama, are the postures or *āsana-s*. The word *āsana* means "easy, comfortable": "To be motionless for a long time with no effort is called an *āsana*." (*Yoga Darshana* II, 46.)

It means that before attempting the postures of yoga, one should place one's body in an easy, relaxed position. Yoga does not encourage violent and exhausting exercises. It is its theory that the largest percentage of energy should be secured for the minimum percentage of energy expended. We should get a maximum dividend for the smal-

44

lest investment. We do not intend to build up large muscles but increase our *vital index,* which, according to *Yoga Mimānsa,* Vol. II, No. 4, is obtained by "dividing a man's lung capacity by his weight. Everyone knows how essential oxygen is to life. This oxygen is made available to the system by the lungs. Hence the vitality of an individual mainly depends upon his lung capacity. The weight of the man represents the bulk of the tissues that his lungs are called upon to vitalize. Thus lung capacity (the vitalizing agent) divided by the weight to be vitalized gives the vital index." To this I would like to add that the *vital index* would also depend on how an individual *uses his lung capacity.*

In an *āsana* the body is placed in a relaxed position with the centres of the body in a geometric figure which is characteristic of a certain manifestation or species of living being in the natural world. Thus many of the *āsana-s* are named after certain natural phenomena (like the sun) or living beings (like the lion, tortoise and peacock). When the geometric figure represented by the centres of the body in a yoga posture is that of a particular species (like that of a relaxing cat's for instance) we become part of the cosmic entity which manifests itself in that species and receive certain benefits. When the lion yawns with his tongue stretched out, or the horse rears to flush his limbs with blood, they are carrying out beneficial actions which may be duplicated by man in an *āsana.*

According to Yoga philosophy, in the beginning Primal Force (electricity) created all things by assuming the characteristic geometric shape *(āsana)* of a particular species or element of Nature. Shiva himself (Primal Force) created all the things by assuming with his substance the geometric shapes and number of charges of electricity in them (which give the vital centres) of each characteristic living or inanimate thing. Thus was the world created by the different geometrical and numerical arrangements of electric charges.

We really owe the manifest world to the *āsana-s.* It is their basic geometrical structure. And it is the primal force *(shiva)* who made the manifest world the beginning by assuming himself, with his own body, the different geometric shapes (with the vital centres) of all living and non-living things.

45

The number of *āsana-s* or yoga postures assumed by Shiva to create the world was eighty-four times one hundred thousand. Of these, eighty-four are generally practiced in India, and have been described in our ancient texts, and thirty-three are said to be specially important.

In this chapter I shall describe some of the easy postures for beginners, which are equally good for men and women, and the aged and young. Even a short practice of ten minutes each day will be beneficial for the practitioner. It takes about a fortnight to learn basic exercises which can be practiced throughout one's life.

In the beginning one should confine oneself to the simple postures described in this chapter. They make the body flexible, achieve better co-ordination between mind and body, and bring the more difficult ones within the student's reach. One should never strain while practicing these postures; with practice, one should be able to remain in them for longer periods than is at first possible. The exercises should be performed in a well ventilated room, upon a rug, mattress or blanket stretched on the floor.

Breathings play as important a part in the performance of yoga as concentration does. To derive maximum benefits in minimum time, coordination of breathing and mind with each movement of muscle while performing a yoga posture is essential. During a single posture, the student has to inhale at one position, he has to exhale at another position, and he is required to retain breath at a certain position. He must also know when to start inhaling and exhaling and when to stop. In addition he must know the duration of inhalation, exhalation and retention of breath while performing the posture. The place of concentration on different parts of the body and various glands should also be learned. In the performance of a single posture, the place, duration and intensity of concentration changes. Students who are not careful in coordinating breathing and mind through concentration while performing yoga postures progress slowly and sometimes they may not progress at all. Therefore it is advisable that the guidance of an expert in yoga (a *guru*) be obtained at the earliest possible opportunity. One should start the beginner's yoga postures at home to be followed by the main postures and finally the advanced course. While practicing the main and advanced yoga courses, the student should keep in touch with the teacher three or four times a month at least in order to maintain steady progress.

The process and duration of breathing and concentration has been explained in this book with each separate posture.

10. YOGA POSTURES FOR

BEGINNERS

i. THE POSTURE OF THE HARE

Purpose:

1) To relax the spine after contracting and stretching it.
2) To give a massage to the abdominal viscera.
3) To slow and make steady the pulsing of the heart.
4) To send a new supply of blood to brain, eyes and other parts of the head.
5) To relieve tension from the spine, ankles and back of the neck.

Technique:

(Illustration 2). Sit on a soft rug with knees and shanks on the floor, kneeling position, sitting on your heels, and the palms under the soles of your feet. Now, breathing in deeply, bend backward, contracting the spine. One should bend backward only as far as one can do so with convenience. When the breath is full, start exhaling, and at the same time, bend forward slowly, arching the vertebrae of spine. Go on shifting weight from the feet to the knees 'til the top of the head is on the floor and the forehead is touching the knees. Keep the hips about two and a half feet above the heels. While holding this position for about ten to thirty seconds, breathe in and out in the normal way. Concentrate on the space between the two eye-brows to send *prāna* (the body's vital energy) to the pineal gland to stimulate and activate it. Now start taking in a deep breath and raise the head until original sitting posture is reached; and continue bending backwards until the spine is once more contracted and arched. To begin with this exercise may be repeated three times.

Benefits:

This posture is a good substitute for the Head Stand *(Sirshāsana).* Besides giving one the benefits of the Head Stand, which sends a new

48

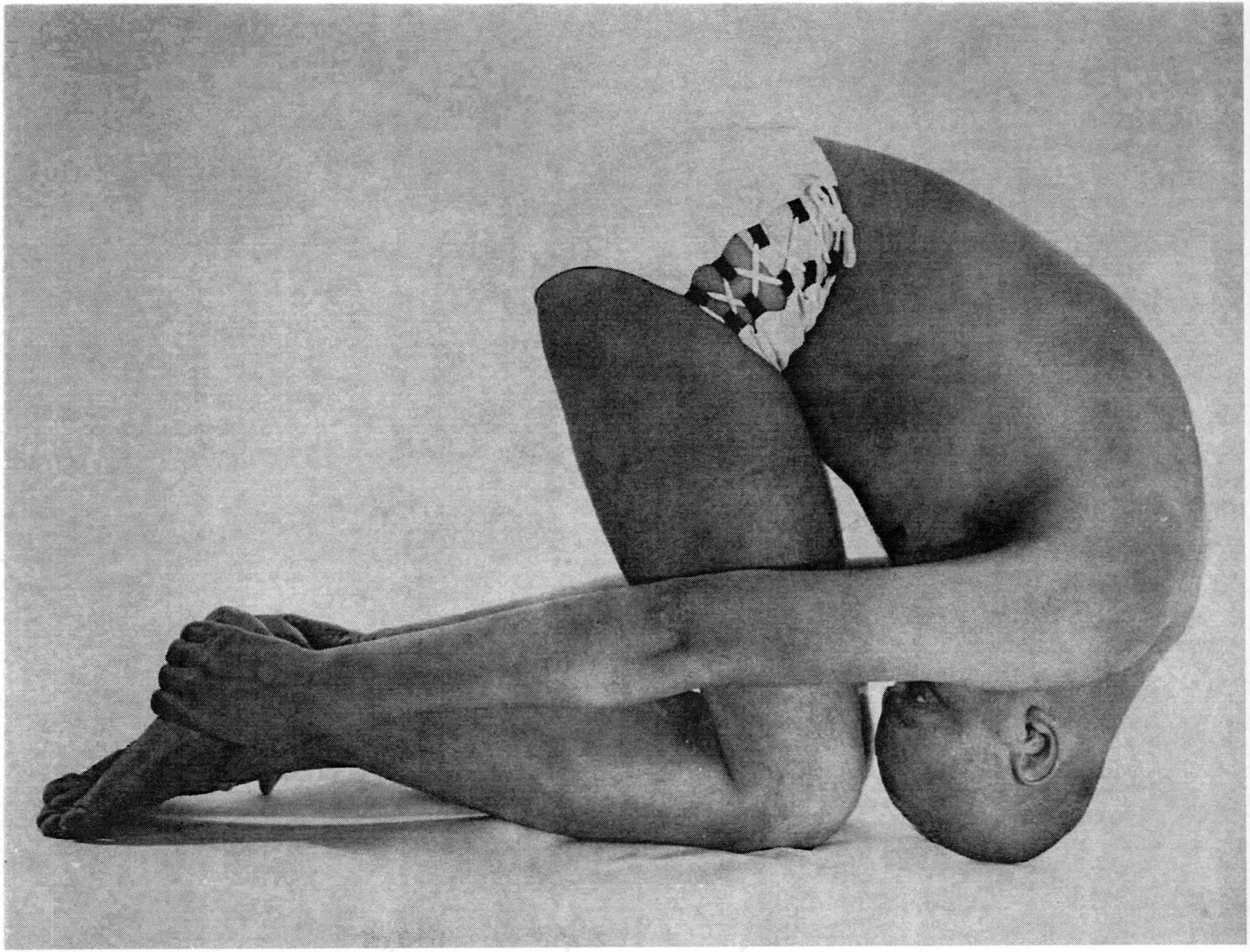

Illustration 2. The Posture of the Hare

supply of blood to the brain, it stimulates and exercises the pancreas, kidneys and liver as well as the muscles of the abdomen. Stretching and contracting the spine, it has a wonderful effect on it afterwards. It stimulates the circulation of blood in the entire body and rests the heart since it does not have to pump so much blood to the upper regions of the body when the head is on the floor. At the same time the heart does not have to work so hard to pump blood from the lower part of the body to the ventricles. This posture improves memory, eyesight and the power of hearing. After a few weeks practice of this posture, many of my students reported to me that their scalps felt more healthy and their hair had grown more thick and black.

II. EXERCISING THE WAIST

Purpose:

1) To achieve co-ordination between the mind and breath.
2) To bring "steadiness" to the nerves and mind.
3) To develop mental concentration.
4) To stretch and strengthen the waist muscles.

Technique:

(Illustration 3). Lie on the back. Keep the spine straight, with arms on either side of body and palms on the floor. Now start inhaling and, without bending the knees, raise the left leg up until it is vertical, or at least as vertical as possible. Breathing in and raising of the leg to vertical should begin and stop at the same time and occupy eight heart beats, or 'till one counts eight. Retain the breath and the leg in the vertical position for the count of six. Now begin to exhale and bring the leg down to the floor for the count of eight, or eight heart beats.

Now take in a normal deep breath and while breathing out relieve the tension from legs and hands, and turn palms to face the ceiling.

To start with, this movement should be done three times, first with the left and then the right leg. While exercising, concentrate on the navel.

50

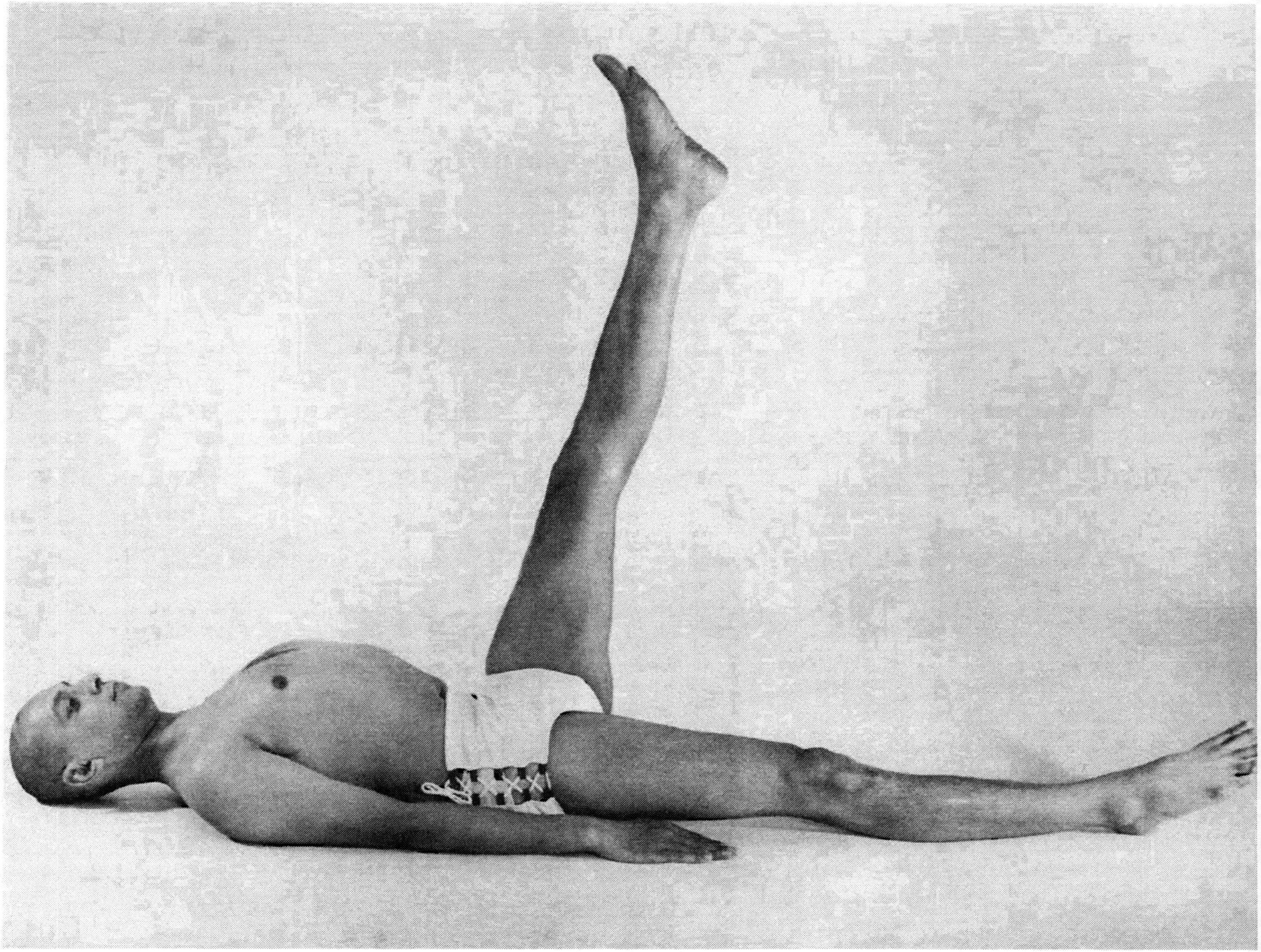

Illustration 3. Exercising the Waist

Benefits:

This exercise stretches the body, exercises the abdominal muscle, and gives one a quickened exhilarated feeling.

Many of my students in the United States of eighty and over start with this exercise. When they become more nimble and flexible, they practice the other postures, which appear difficult in the beginning.

III. *ARDHA-SALABHĀSANA:*
THE HALF LOCUST POSTURE

Purpose:

1) To prevent constipation.
2) To relieve tension in the spine.
3) To strengthen spine and abdominal muscles.

Technique:

(Illustration 4). Lie on the floor, resting on right cheek. Keep arms stretched on either side of the body, palms facing the ceiling. Breathing in, raise left leg without bending the knee, keeping the right leg stiff. The breath should be full when the leg is fully raised. One should retain it for six heart beats. Then lower the leg, breathing out, with perfect ease, and not in fits and jerks. While exercising concentrate on the lower part of the spine. Time of inhalation, retention and exhalation should be the same as given in previous exercise, that is eight heart-beats (or the counting of eight), and six and eight heart-beats.

Now lie on the left cheek and repeat the process with the right leg, while keeping the other stiff.

This exercise is not found in the original yoga texts, but is a modern extension of their principles. The exercise is named after the Sanscrit name for "locust" — *Salabha.*

Benefits:

This exercise tones up the muscles of the pelvis and abdomen. It strengthens the intestinal walls and increases supply of nerve-force to them. It immediately activates ascending, descending and traverse colons and is excellent for flatulence.

52

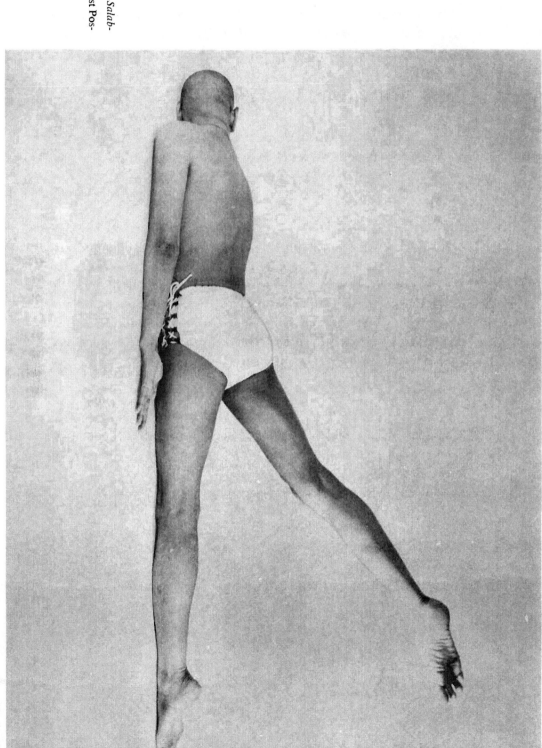

Illustration 4. *Ardha-Salab-hāsana*: The Half Locust Posture

The spine is pulled anteriorly and every vertebra and its ligaments are exercised. The thirty-one pairs of spinal nerves of the spine are stimulated. The deep muscles of the back are also activated through an increase in blood supply.

IV. EXERCISING THE ABDOMEN

Purpose:

1) To strengthen the legs and the abdominal muscles.
2) To stretch the spine up to the top-most vertebrae.
3) To strengthen the organs of digestion, assimilation and elimination.

Technique:

(Illustration 5). Lie on the floor on the back and taking in a half breath, raise both legs together about two to three inches above the floor. Keep toes out-stretched and both legs stiff. See that the legs do not tremble. Keep the position from six to thirty seconds according to convenience, breathing in and out in the normal way, and concentrating on the spine. One should feel that each vertebra has become separated, one from the other, from down up.

Benefits:

This exercise prepares one for the more difficult postures by strengthening the spine and making it more flexible. It draws fresh supplies of blood to it and has a refreshing effect on the whole body. In my classes here in New York, students of all ages are amazed how refreshed they feel after doing the exercise, although they have arrived tired from a full day's work only a few minutes previously.

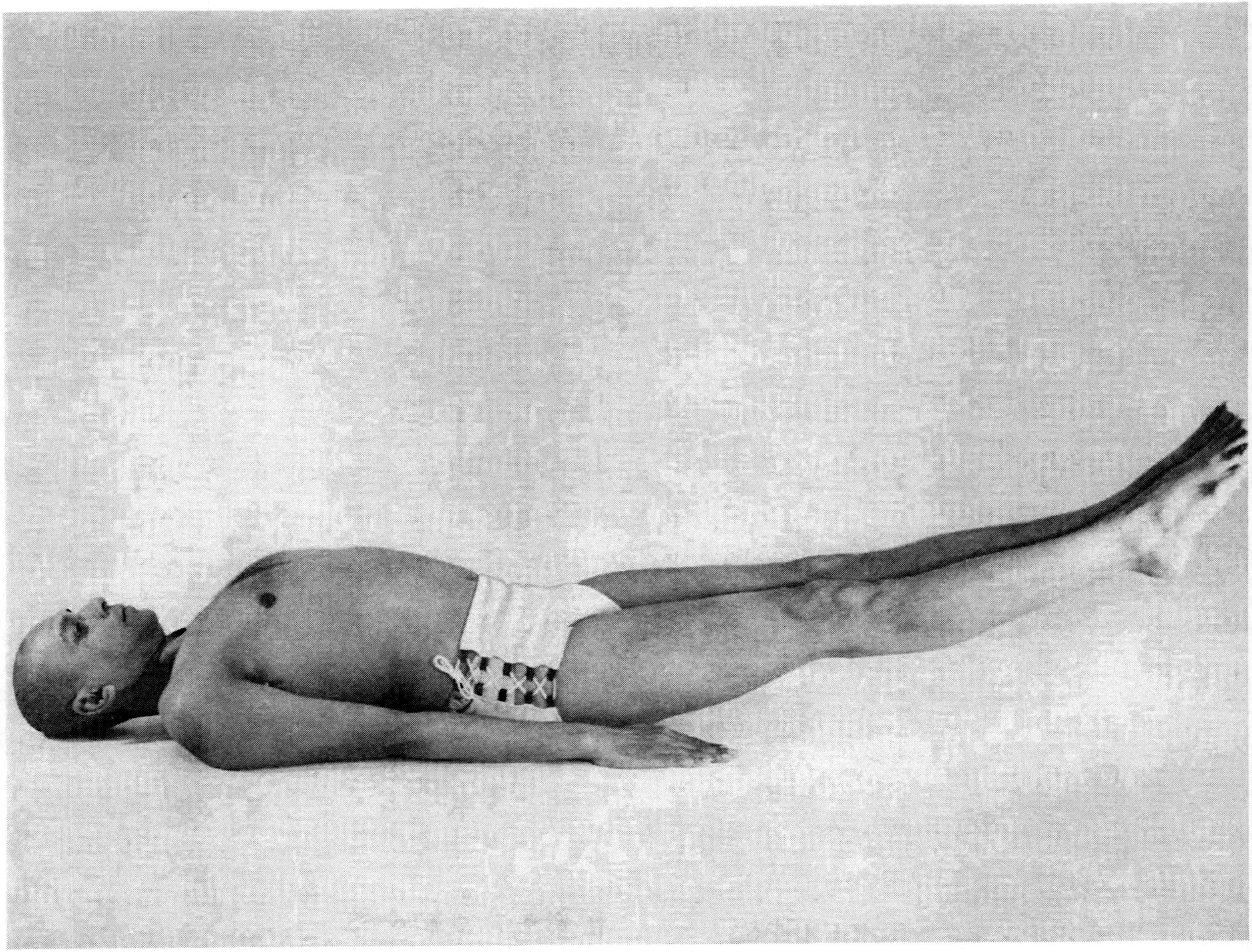

Illustration 5.   Exercising
the Abdomen

v. *ARDHA-MATSYĀSANA:*
THE HALF FISH POSTURE

Purpose:

1) To strengthen the chest case, collar bones and shoulders, and broaden the chest.
2) To strengthen and increase the capacity of the lungs.
3) To strengthen the larynx (wind box) and the trachea (windpipe).

Technique:

(Illustration 6). Lie on the floor keeping the spine straight and the legs out-stretched. Bend the legs now by pulling in the heels to touch buttocks. Assisted by the elbows, arch neck backwards as shown in illustration, until the back of the head touches the floor. The spine is bent like an arch. Now hold neck with the palms of the hands, taking care that the elbows or the back do not touch the floor. The weight of the body should be solely supported by the head, the buttocks and the soles of the feet. In this position breathe in for eight heart-beats (or until one counts eight), retain the breath for six heart-beats, and breathe out for ten heart-beats. While inhaling and exhaling concentrate on the thyroid glands situated in the neck. (Figure 2, p. 34).

To begin with the exercise should be repeated three times only.

Benefits:

This exercise banishes tension, cramps and stiffness in the neck. It stimulates the function of the thyroid and parathyroid glands (whose important functions were explained in a previous chapter), as well as the pituitary and pineal glands. It may be practiced after the Pan-Physical Posture or Shoulder Stand *(Sarvangāsana)* which is shown in Illustration 13.

This exercise improves the voice and breathing capacity to a tremendous extent. Many of my students who were singers found an almost miraculous improvement in their singing after two or three weeks practice of the Half Fish Posture.

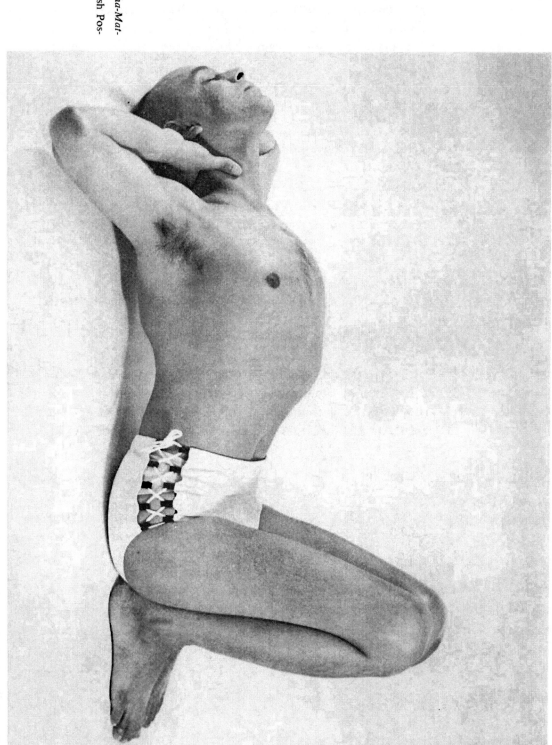

Illustration 6. *Ardha-Mat-syāsana*: The Half Fish Posture

vi. *ARDHA-VAKRĀSANA I:*
THE HALF SPINAL TWIST I

Purpose:

1) To twist each vertebra in the spine on its base separately, first to the left and then to the right.
2) To eliminate pressure on the cartilages between each pair of vertebrae.
3) To exercise the long muscles of the back.
4) To exercise nerves and muscles of the neck.

Technique:

(Illustration 7). Sit down on the floor with both legs stretched out in front. Now keeping the left leg straight, bend the right leg at the knee and drawing it towards the chest, place sole of the foot on floor on left side of the other knee. Grasp right ankle with the left hand keeping the left arm on the right side of the right leg, and right waist with right hand.

Now start breathing in for four heart beats (or while counting four) and twist trunk to the right as far as possible. Retain the breath in this posture for six heart-beats and then untwist spine to its original position, exhaling for a period of eight heart-beats. While inhaling and exhaling concentrate on the shoulder towards which you have moved your face.

Stretch both legs again and bend left leg at the knee and place sole of the foot on right side of other knee. Grasping left ankle with right hand and left waist with left hand, repeat the whole process on the left side.

The exercise is named after the Sanscrit word *vakra* which means twisted.

Benefits:

This exercise balances the positive and negative forces in the body (which were explained in Chapter 4) and increases breathing capacity and the body's elasticity. It strengthens ribs, shoulders and spine and affords immunity from lumbago and other muscular rheumatisms of the back muscles. The spinal nerve roots and the whole sympathetic nervous system are toned up. The ligaments attached to the vertebrae are stretched and exercised, and their blood supply increased.

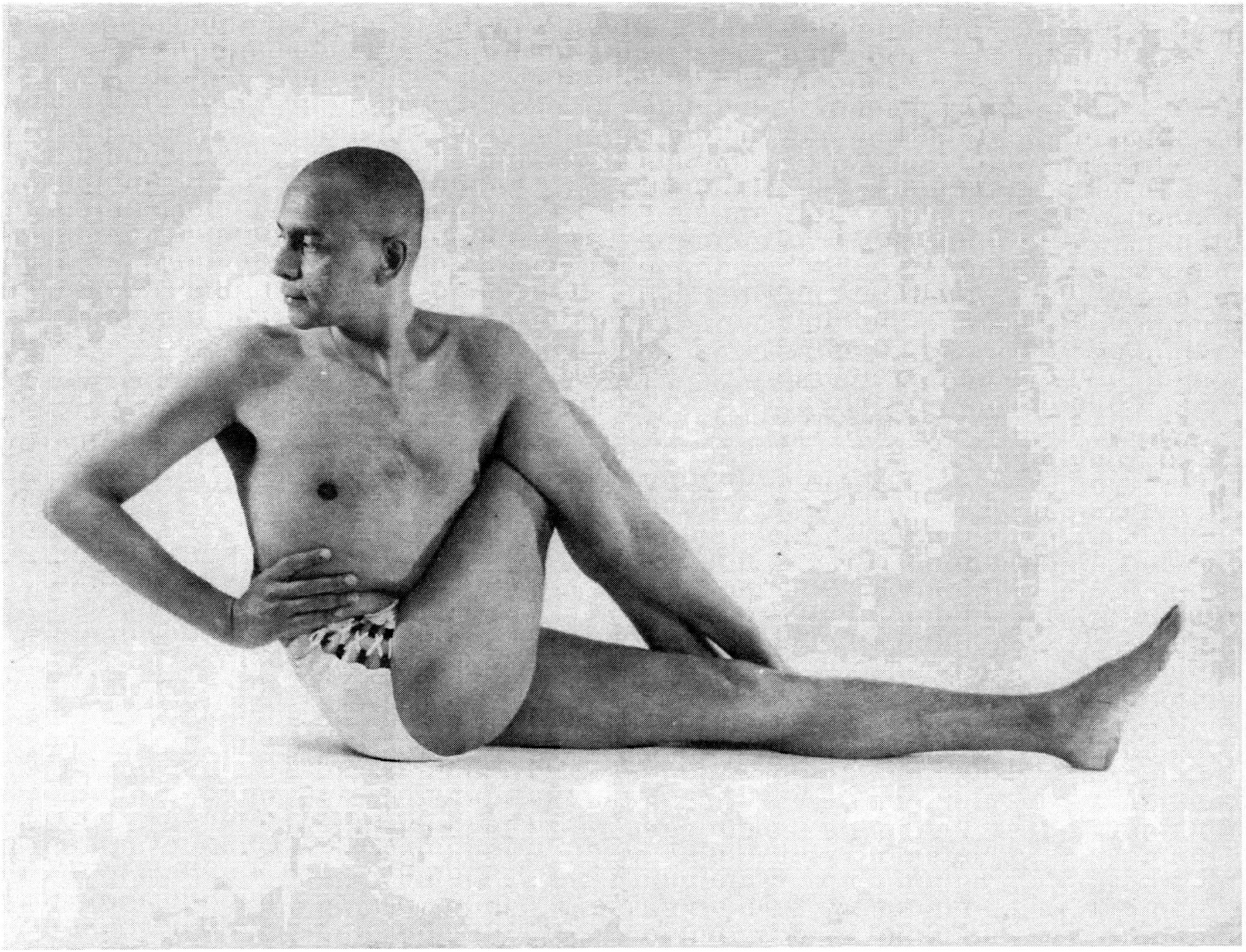

Illustration 7. *Ardha-Vak-*
rāsana I: The Half Spinal
Twist I

VII. *SIMHĀSANA:*

THE LION POSTURE

Purpose:

1) To exercise the internal organs of throat (tonsils, etc.) and the tongue.
2) To tone up the auditory system (ears).
3) To exercise the ligaments joining the jaws.
4) To strengthen the diaphram and the intestines.

Technique:

(Illustration 8). Sit down with legs bent and top of feet on the floor. Grasp knees firmly with both hands. Now start exhaling and protruding the tongue at the same time. One should try to extend tongue 'till its tip touches the chin. At this point hold the breath for as long as it is convenient and contract the abdominal muscles inward and then upward towards the thorax, and with eyes wide open (to imitate the lion's fierceness) concentrate on the space between the two eyebrows. Now start inhaling, letting the tongue go in and relaxing the abdominal muscles.

After two or three normal breaths, the process may be repeated. To start with, do it only once.

The exercise is named after the Sanscrit word for lion, *Simha,* since the student imitates the lion when he thrusts his tongue out fully with his jaws wide open.

Benefits:

This exercise is beneficial for singers, radio-announcers, public speakers, etc. It strengthens all vital parts of the throat including vocal cords and uvula. Many of my students who were singers wrote to me their voices had greatly improved after practicing this exercise.

60

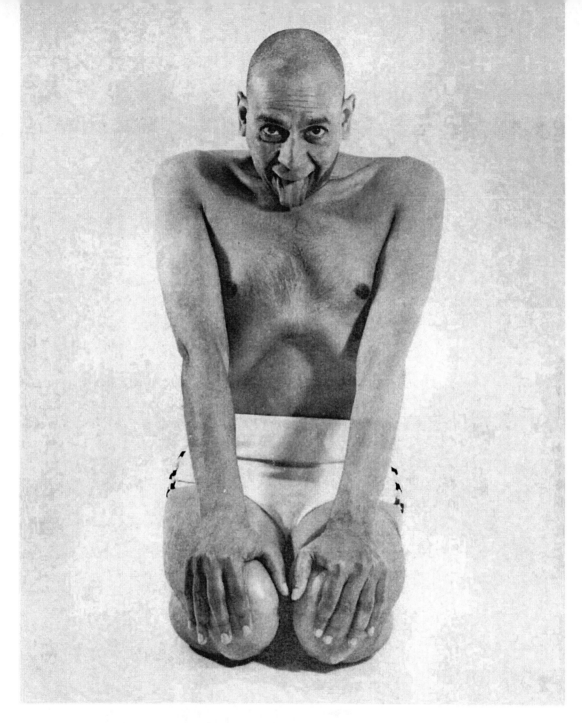

Illustration 8.   *Simhāsana:* The Lion Posture

VIII. POSTURE FOR RELIEVING GAS
FROM INTESTINES AND COLON

Purpose:

1) To help natural peristaltic action in the colon.
2) To improve breathing and bring steadiness and will-power to the mind.
3) To relieve the intestines and colon of gas.

Technique:

(Illustration 9). Stand straight on the left foot and bend right leg from the knee (with hands on shank as shown in the illustration) until the knee touches the chest and the heel, the lower part of thigh. Draw in the ankle with the right hand so that the raised thigh applies pressure on the ascending colon. Hold this posture for half a minute and concentrate on the ascending colon. The body should not shake or move.

Now repeat the process with the left foot and concentrate on the descending colon.

Benefits:

This exercise activates the ascending and descending colons, and strengthens the arches of the feet. It increases will power through concentration, and develops steadiness in the breath and nerves. ·

Many of my students have told me that, after this exercise, their bowels have been functioning normally for the first time in years.

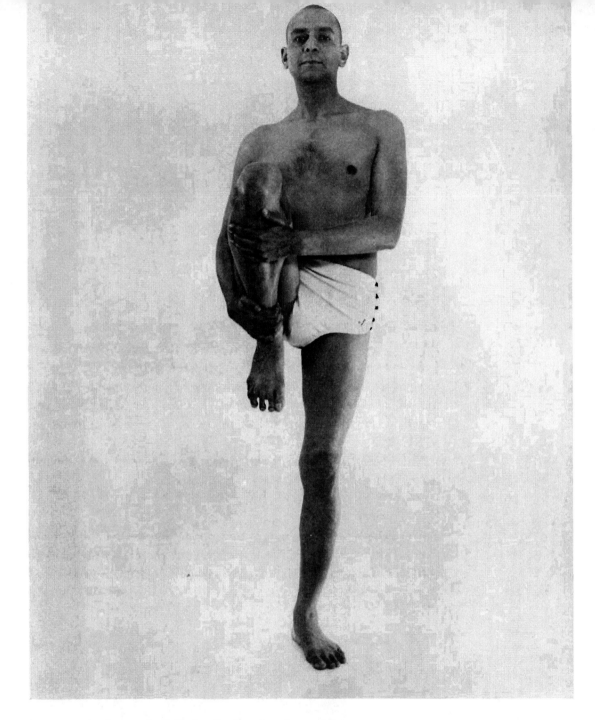

Illustration 9. Posture for Relieving Gas from Intestines and Colon

IX. APPLYING TRANSVERSE PRESSURE
ON THE SPINE

Purpose:

1) To apply transverse pressure on the spine.
2) To banish dejection and a sense of inferiority.
3) To bring relaxation to body and mind.

Technique:

(Illustration 10). Stand erect on left foot and bend right leg back with knee downwards so that the heel touches the right buttock. Hold on to right foot with right hand. Throw the left hand upwards towards the ceiling. Feel that you are about to touch the ceiling with your fingers. Concentrate on the ceiling. Keep the body straight and STRETCH.

Now repeat the process standing on the right foot and stretching the right hand.

Benefits:

This exercise brings thousands of tiny muscles into action and activates them. It stretches, contracts and then relaxes the nerves and muscles of the spinal column. It makes the body flexible, light and well balanced.

64

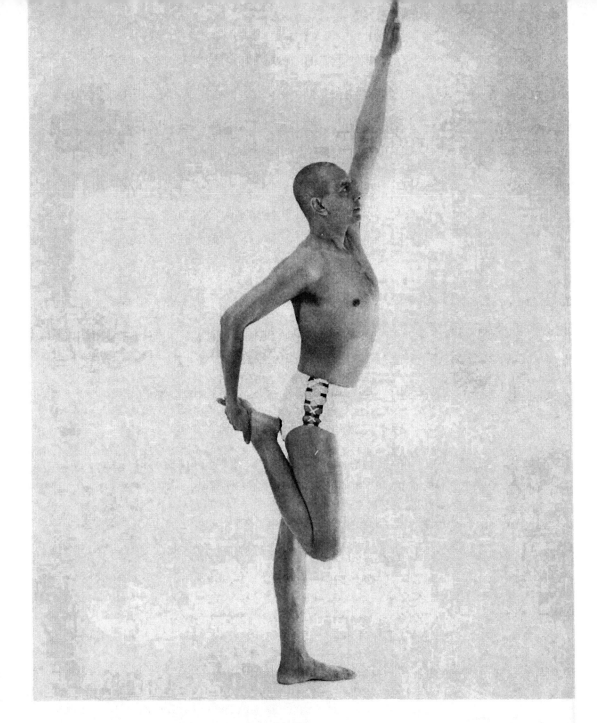

Illustration 10.   Applying Transverse Pressure on the Spine

11. THE MAIN POSTURES
OF YOGA

x. *BHUJANGĀSANA.*
THE COBRA POSTURE

Purpose:

1) To exercise the deep muscles of the back.
2) To prevent the internal organs from dropping.
3) To give excellent natural shape to the spine.

Technique:

(Illustration 11). Lie down with arms on either side of body with elbows raised and with forehead and the palms just below shoulders touching the floor. Feet and toes are stretched out stiff behind with the soles upward.

Now, breathing in slowly, raise the head from the neck and bend it backwards as far as it will go, with the chin thrust out. Next contract the muscles of the back and raise the chest from the floor with the help of some leverage from the arms. The curving of the back should not be brought about suddenly, but gradually, and while doing this concentrate on each vertebra's action. Feel the curving of the vertebrae one by one downwards. The more deliberately this is done, the more easily is the pressure of the spine traveling downwards felt. Throughout this exercise it is important that the body from the navel to the toes should remain touching the floor. Concentration should be on the spine moving downward along the point of pressure in the spine as the head is being raised. While at top of pose, concentration should be on the solar plexus, then, as pose is relaxed and head is lowered, concentration should follow the point of pressure back up the spine.

While in this posture one may breathe in and out, but advanced students retain the breath. Hold the posture for five seconds or less.

Now begin to efface the spinal curve slowly and gradually while breathing out — first the lumbar, then the thoracic and finally the

66

Illustration 11. *Bhujaṅgāsa-na:* The Cobra Posture

cervical curves, and feel the pressure being relieved from each vertebra which now travels upwards until the spine is in a horizontal line once more and the forehead touches the ground.

To begin with, this exercise should be practiced three to five times, and the period of retention may be increased from five seconds to longer as the spine gets accustomed to it. It should be noted that in the beginning the rising thorax is supported by the arms but that with practice the muscles of the back alone will accomplish the process. When in this full position the student may with the aid of his arms and deep muscles of back work the lumbar region. Abdominal muscles including the two recti are stretched and pressure is increased in the abdomen.

This exercise is named after the Sanscrit *bhujanga* or *cobra* since it resembles the hooded snake's rising when it is excited.

Caution. In the beginning do not attempt any form of breath control. Let it flow naturally.

Benefits:

This posture unfolds the latent power in the various plexuses and nerve centers. It is specially good for women; for toning up the muscles of the chest, breasts, ovaries, uterus and womb. It is a powerful tonic. While the thorax is raised all these parts are drawn upwards and flushed with huge quantities of blood; revitalizing them. The muscles of the back are also exercised.

The regular practice of this posture is said to develop confidence and courage. When the thorax is raised the blood is squeezed out from the kidneys, but as soon as it is lowered blood flushes back into them and carries away all deposits which are ultimately excreted.

XI. *SALABHĀSANA:*
THE LOCUST POSTURE

Purpose:

1) To strengthen vertebrae of the lumbar and sacral regions.
2) To increase blood supply to liver, pancreas and kidneys.
3) To strengthen abdominal muscles.

68

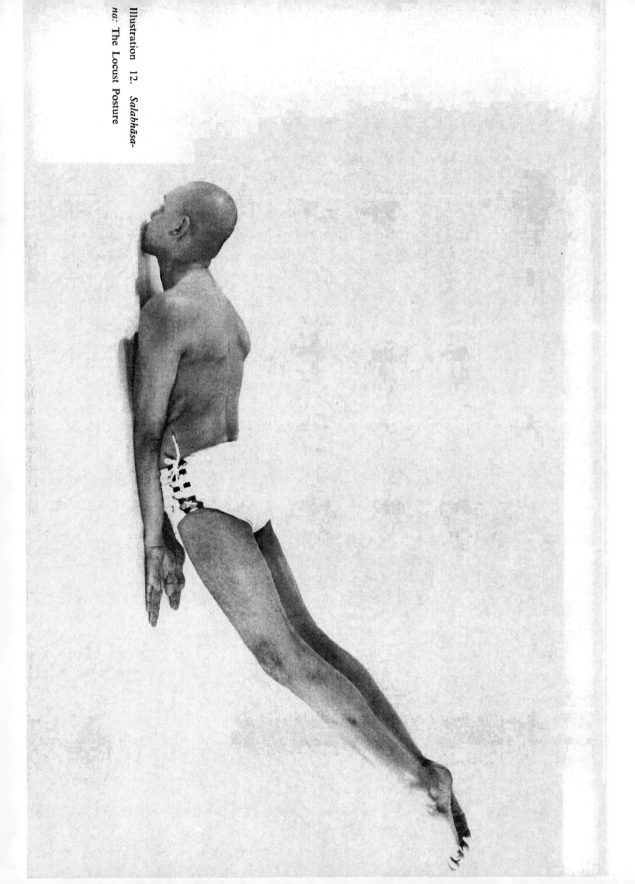

Illustration 12. *Salabhāsa-na:* The Locust Posture

Technique:

(Illustration 12). Lie on a soft rug or folded blanket with chin resting on it, the body straight and clenched hands on either side. The shoulders and back of fists touch the rug. Now take a deep breath, hold it, and stiffening the body raise the legs up, supporting weight on chest and hands. Keep shanks, thighs and toes in a straight line and note that the sacrum too is partly raised. Concentrate on the solar plexus during this exercise.

When the breath can be held no longer, lower the legs and relax. When the breath is normal again, repeat the process. Although this is the only *āsana* in yoga where the lower part of the body is suddenly raised, the movement though sudden should be smoothly done.

Beginner may remain in this posture for five to ten seconds, and it may be repeated two to four times according to the capacity of the practitioner. It will be noted that in this exercise the lower part of the body which remains passive in the Cobra Posture *(Bhujangāsana)* is exercised, while the upper part which is exercised by it, remains passive.

Benefits:

The Cobra Posture described in the previous exercise develops the upper half of the body, while this posture develops the lower half. It stimulates blood circulation to the intestines, furthers digestion and elimination, and prevents constipation. By increasing internal abdominal pressure, it strengthens the liver, pancreas and kidneys and stimulates the digestive glands. Due to retention of breath in the full posture, lung capacity is increased.

XII. *SARVĀNGĀSANA:*
THE PAN-PHYSICAL POSTURE OR SHOULDER STAND

Purpose:

1) To rejuvenate the body.
2) To strengthen the spine, shoulders and neck.
3) To rest several parts of the body like the heart and the veins of the legs, which are not usually rested.

70

Illustration 13. *Sarvāngāsana:* The Pan-Physical Posture

Technique:

(Illustration 13). Lie in a well ventilated room on the back with hands on either side and breathing in a little raise both legs up together smoothly to vertical with toes stretched. The action may be performed in easy stages, first to thirty degrees between legs and floor, when they may be rested for a few seconds and then to sixty degrees. When the full right angle is reached hold the pose again for a few seconds.

Now holding the hips with both hands, elbows resting on the floor, press chin against the chest (this is the chin-lock) and raise the trunk, hips and legs until they are vertically above the shoulders. To complete chin-lock exert pressure through forearms and hands on trunk so that the chin is well set in the jugular notch. The weight of the body should be well balanced on shoulders, back of neck and elbows and the limbs should not tremble. Breathing slowly and steadily concentrate on the thyroid gland situated in the center of the throat (Figure 2, p. 34). Hold the posture for two to three minutes and then resume supine position on the floor gracefully and smoothly. Many people in India who practice no other postures except this one allow twenty-four minutes for it. When it forms part of other exercises no more than six minutes should be allowed for it.

The exercise is called *Sarva-anga-āsana (Sarvāngāsana)* since in Sanscrit *Sarva* means *whole* and *Anga* means *body*. It is truly a pan-physical posture or one for the *whole body* since it stimulates the thyroid and its secretion of thyroxin hormone which controls the rate of oxidation in the body.

Benefits:

Massage of the thyroid insures constant good health, long life and a prolonged youth. Two or three minutes daily practice, and many of my students eliminated wrinkles from the neck and face, and became the possessors of a fresh and velvety skin.

This posture reduces strain on the heart muscles since they are rested even more than when we are lying in bed. Due to gravitation, blood flows easily to the upper part of the body without imposing on the heart this part of the work of circulation. Through the chin-lock a pool of blood is formed in the neck and upper part of the chest to nourish the lungs, thyroids, tonsils, ear glands, the hilum and thymus. Therefore it is exceptionally good for people whose jobs require much standing.

I, personally, know a yoga student in the Himalayas who is over one hundred years old. He works twelve to eighteen hours every day and his voice is melodious and clear like a young man's. He is brisk and clearheaded with his work and he has all the youthful vigor one could wish for. This is one of the exercises he practices regularly.

XIII. *MATSYĀSANA:*
THE FISH POSTURE

Purpose:

This posture intensifies the benefits derived from the Half Fish Posture. (Exercise V, Page 56).

Technique:

(Illustration 14). Sit down in the Lotus Posture *(Padmāsana)* by placing right foot on the left thigh and the sole of the left foot on the right thigh near the hip joint, as shown in the illustration.

Now bend backwards, with support from the elbows, until the weight of the body is supported by the top of the skull. One should achieve a well-balanced feeling. Now place hands on the feet in the gesture *(mudrā)* depicted in the picture. Breathe slowly and steadily, with very mild retention of the breath for two to three seconds and concentrate on the space between the eyebrows. To discontinue the pose first lie down flat on back and head (by sliding it back) using elbows to relieve tension on neck, and then stretch legs forward. Relax. The posture is named after the Sanscrit *matsya* or fish.

Benefits:

This posture enhances the benefits of the Half Fish Posture (Ardha-Matsyāsana, Exercise V, p. 56). It improves digestion and strengthens the collar bone and the respiratory system, as well as the neck, waist and back. It affords a fine counter-balance to the practice of the Pan-Physical Posture (Sarvāngāsana, Exercise XII, p. 70).

Illustration 14. *Matsyā-sana*: The Fish Posture

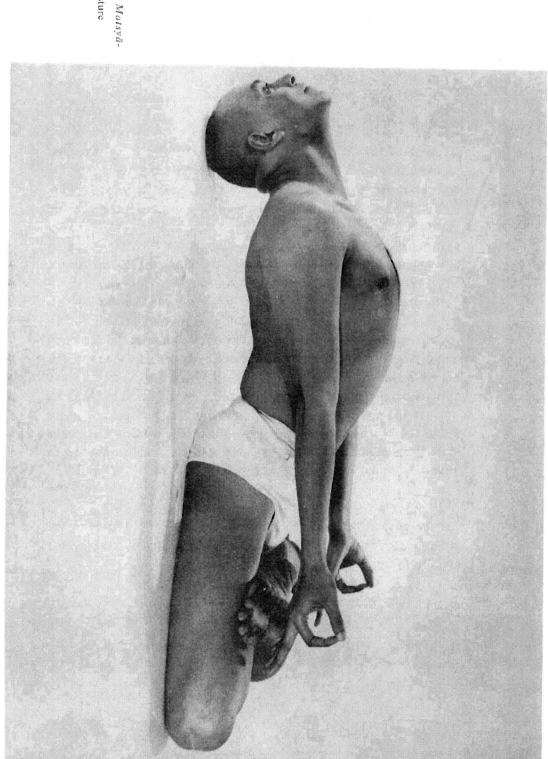

XIV. *ARDHA-VAKRĀSANA II:*
HALF SPINAL TWIST II

Purpose:

1) It intensifies benefits of Half Spinal Twist I.
2) It ensures elasticity of the spinal column.

Technique:

(Illustration 15). Sit down on a soft blanket with both legs stretched forward. Place heel of left foot on the perineum (space between anus and generative organs). Bend the right leg at knee and place sole of foot on the blanket beside left thigh as shown in the illustration, then place your right hand behind your back and catch the ankle of your right leg with your right hand. This action would be facilitated by pressing back knee of right leg with the left arm. Keep this arm straight with wrist to the left of the left knee.

Breathe in and out in this position. Twist neck to right as if to see the nape of the neck. This secures a complete twist to the right for the spinal column. Duration of this posture may ultimately be increased to two minutes, though at first it should occupy no more than three or four seconds.

By reversing leg positions the spine may now be twisted to the left.

When the procedure has been mastered you should breathe in for a count of six while twisting, retain your breath four heart-beats while in the posture, and breathe out for a count of eight while returning to original position. In Sanscrit *vakra* means "twisted."

Benefits:

This posture intensifies benefits of Half Spinal Twist I (Exercise VI, p. 58). By increasing circulation to the spine and the spinal nerves it tones them up. It renders the spine extremely elastic.

Illustration 15. *Ardha-Vakrāsana II:* Half Spinal Twist II

xv. *TRIKONĀSANA:*
TRIANGLE POSTURE

Purpose:

1) To make the spine resilient.
2) To increase height of body.
3) To tone up the nervous system.

Technique:

(Illustration 16, Stages 1-4). Stand erect, keeping feet two and a half feet apart, breathing in and stretch arms to be level with the shoulders, with palms facing floor. Throughout this exercise keep the arms straight. Now bend slowly to the right, exhaling and keeping legs and arms straight, and touch right toes with the right hand. The left arm now points to the ceiling. Move left arm down until it parallels the floor, then swing it to the right as far as possible keeping your eyes at all times on the left palm. Keep this position for three to four seconds, and repeat the action of the arms three or four times. Breathing in again, return to original posture and exhale while bringing the hands down, and the legs together. Next reverse the exercise, bending to the left. The exercise is named after the Sanscrit *trikona* or "triangle."

Benefits:

This exercise gives resilience to the spine and alternately flexes and relaxes the lateral muscles of the back as well as those of hips. It tones up the spinal roots and the abdominal organs. Massaging the bowels, it gives a keen appetite. It is excellent for those who want to increase their height. This is also very beneficial to the eyes.

The vertebrae are moved laterally, and the dorsal muscles which hold vertebrae are also flexed and relaxed.

78

Illustration 16.   (First Stage)   *Trikonāsana:* Triangle Posture

Illustration 16.   (Second Stage)   *Trikonāsana:* Triangle Posture

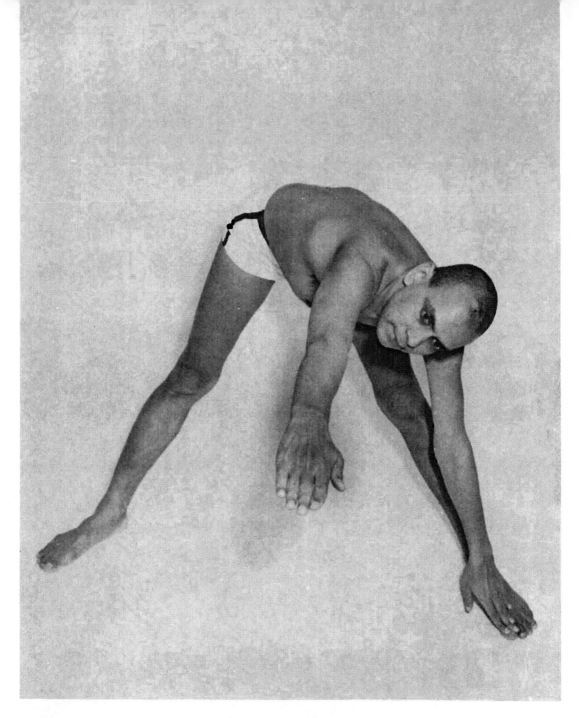

Illustration 16.   (Third Stage)   *Trikonāsana:* Triangle Posture

Illustration 16. (Fourth Stage) *Trikoṇāsana:* Triangle Posture

XVI. *HALĀSANA I:*
THE PLOUGH POSTURE I

Purpose:

1) To stretch the spine, especially the lower part.
2) To prevent accumulation of fat in the abdomen.
3) To strengthen the nervous system.
4) To stimulate the functions of the brain.
5) To prevent softening of the bone of the spine.

Technique:

(Illustration 17 and variation I). Lie on a folded blanket with arms (palms down) on either side of body. Now breathing in, raise hands over head to lie behind it with palms facing the ceiling. Exhale. Now breathing in, raise the legs smoothly through the hip joint until they are vertical keeping legs and knees straight and toes stretched at all times. Then let the lower part of the trunk bend forward in order to lower the legs beyond the head so that the toes touch the floor, while exhaling. The legs should be quite straight and together, with the toes stretched. Breathe slowly and normally in this posture and concentrate on the adrenal glands and the lower part of the spine (Figure 3, p. 130). Now return the legs and arms to original position. The exercise is named *hala-āsana* since the posture resembles the shape of an Indian plough. In Sanscrit *hala* means a "plough."

Benefits:

This posture keeps the spine fully elastic, develops strong abdominal muscles, and through contracting abdominal viscera, is excellent for constipation when these conditions are due to weakness of abdominal muscles or of the nerves that control the process of digestion.

Through the stretching and contraction of each and every vertebra, and its ligaments and nerves they are nourished with extra blood. It also prevents softening of the bone.

This *āsana* reduces the waistline and tones up the digestive organs, the muscles of the lumbar region and neck, the liver and the spleen.

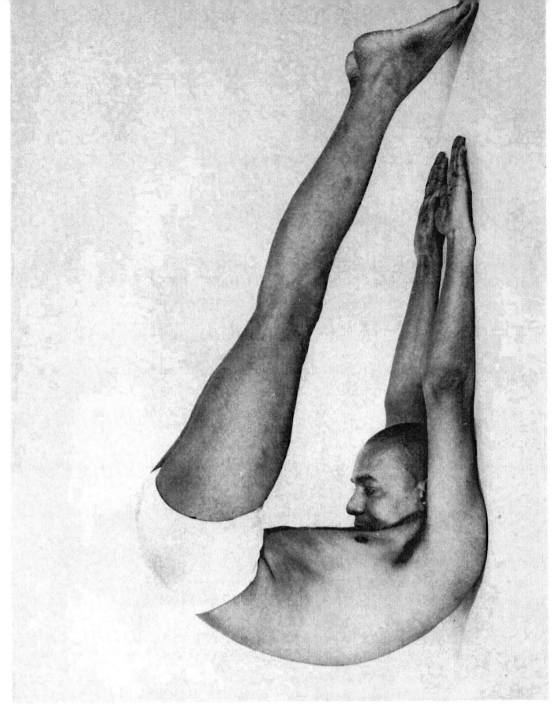

Illustration 17. *Halāsana I*:
The Plough Posture I

Illustration 17. (First Variation) *Halāsana I*: The Plough Posture I

In fact, it is the prescribed posture for an enlarged liver or spleen, when the enlargement is not great.

The Locust Posture *(Salabhāsana,* Exercise XI, p. 68), subjects the exterior side of the spine to compression and the inside to tension, whereas this posture puts tension on the outside and the compression on the inner side.

Tension, fatigue and weariness disappear in a few seconds through this *āsana* since a fresh supply of blood is flushed into the spinal regions.

XVII. *PASCHIMATANĀSANA:* OR THE POSTERIOR STRETCHING POSTURE

Purpose:

1) To stretch hamstring muscles (posterior muscles of shank), and in fact posterior muscles of the whole leg.
2) To bend spine anteriorly and stretch posterior muscles of thorax.
3) To balance the negative and positive currents in the spine.

Technique:

(Illustration 18). Lie on the floor on a folded blanket with the legs stretched out. Take a deep breath and raise arms half-circle until they rest on the blanket on the other side of the head. Now raise arms and thorax into sitting position and, exhaling, bend forward to catch the big toes with a hooked forefinger. Breathe in and out in this position and concentrate on the spine. To start with one may remain in this position for two or three seconds. Now inhale and resume the supine position smoothly.

In Sanscrit *paschima* means the *posterior* and the root *tan,* to *stretch. Paschimatāna* therefore means *stretching the posterior* (muscles).

Benefits:

This posture contracts the front abdominal muscles and strengthens them.It is an excellent means of improving the digestive processes.

It stretches the posterior muscles of the body, especially the hamstring muscles below the pits of knees and it strengthens the muscles and nerves of the lumbosacral region.

86

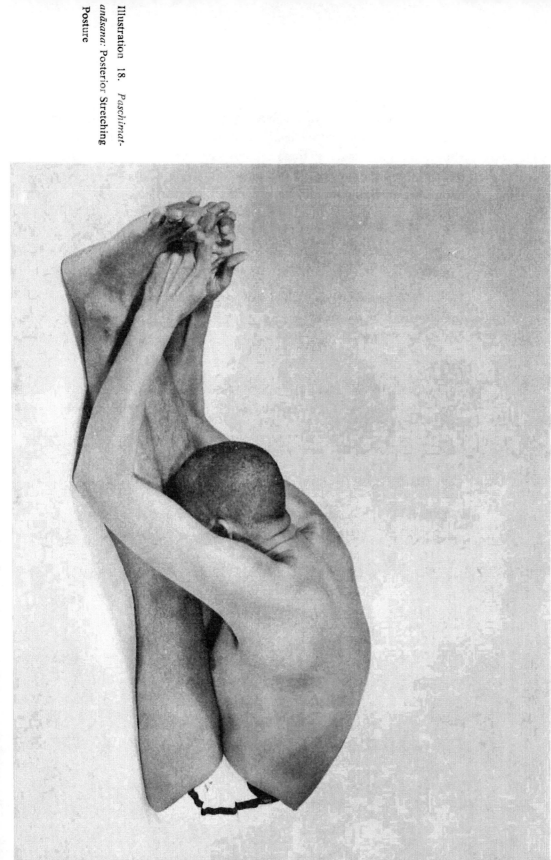

Illustration 18. *Paschimat-anāsana*: Posterior Stretching Posture

When practiced for over an hour this position is known to bring *Anāhata Dhavani* or *the subtle sound* to the student's hearing. And it also rouses the *kundalini* force which was described in Chapter 4. But this exercise must be performed with discretion since it has been found that over-practice may have ill effects.

XVIII. *VIRĀSANA:*
THE HERO POSTURE

Purpose:

1) To balance the flow of prāna *(vital force)* in the body.
2) To straighten the spine.
3) To strengthen arms and wrists.

Technique:

(Illustration 19). Sit down on a folded blanket with legs in front. Now bend right leg at the knee and place foot on left thigh near the hip joint. The right knee should rest on the blanket. Now bend left leg to place the foot under the thigh (as shown in illustration) so the body is resting on it. While in this position breathe in and out normally. Hands should be in the position shown in the illustration.

Benefits:

Many of the benefits gained from the Lotus Posture *(Padmāsana)*, (Exercise XIII, p. 74) may also be derived from this posture. It relieves pressure from the abdominal region and rests the digestive organs. It increases appetite. It also relieves tension in the muscles of the ankle and in muscles around the shoulder blades.

Deep breathing and "concentration" *(pratyāhāra,* Ch. 13) may be practiced in this posture.

Illustration 19. *Virāsana:* The Hero Posture

12. POSTURES FOR ADVANCED STUDENTS

The exercises meant for advanced students should, as far as possible, be practiced after proper instruction from a teacher. Because no two individuals are alike in physique, age, vitality and psychological background, these factors must be taken into consideration in deciding when an individual is fit to start the advanced postures described in this chapter.

An average student takes six months to prepare himself for the advanced postures under the guidance of a teacher. Since there is a great improvement in general health through the earlier exercises I have noted that students are often in a hurry to study the advanced postures. They should be more patient. It is only the thorough mastery of the earlier ones that can make a safe basis for the practice of the more difficult postures.

xix. *SIRSHĀSANA:*
HEAD STAND AND
HEAD STAND IN LOTUS POSTURE

Purpose.

1) To improve powers of concentration and memory.
2) To relax the heart and tone up the body.
3) To increase will-power and self-confidence.
4) To arouse the dormant faculties of the mind and body.

Technique:

(Illustration 20, Stages 1-7). Spread a soft rug on the floor and resting on knees make a finger lock by entwining fingers. Place hands firmly on the floor and using the two elbows for support and the arms to balance the body, place head in the finger lock. (The finger lock can also be applied further up the head — as shown in illustration). Now straighten knees, balance the body on forearms and toes, and raise toes from

Illustration 20. (First Stage)
Sirshāsana: Head Stand

Illustration 20. (Second Stage) *Sirshāsana:* Head Stand

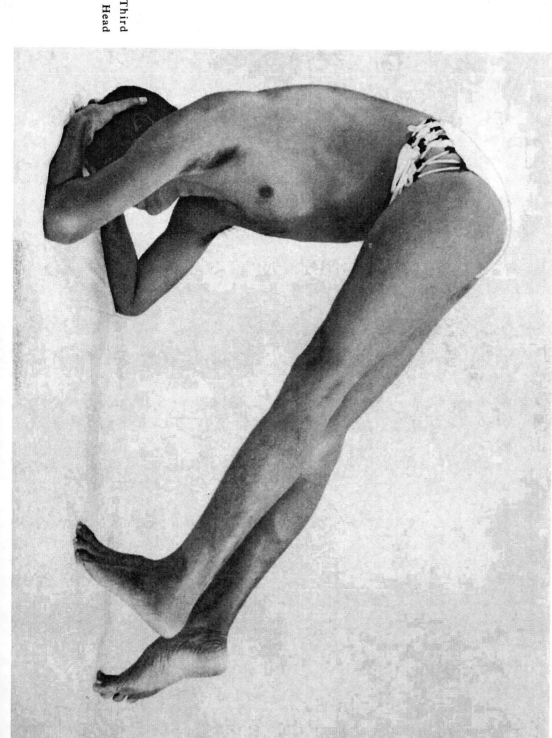

Illustration 20. (Third Stage) *Sirshāsana:* Head Stand

Illustration 20.   (Fourth Stage)   *Sirshāsana:* Head Stand

94

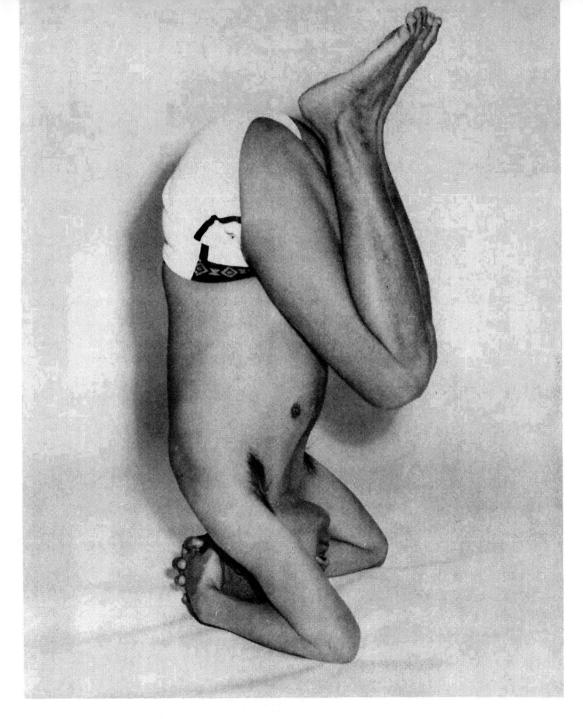

Illustration 20.   (Fifth Stage)   *Sirshāsana:* Head Stand

Illustration 20. (Sixth Stage) *Sirshāsana:* Head Stand

Illustration 20.   (Seventh Stage)   *Sirshāsana:* Head Stand

the rug. Bend knees so that they touch the chest, and the heels the buttocks. Then raise legs slowly so that the feet are over the hips, and thrust them vertically up. This is the Head Stand.

Now place the right foot in groin of left thigh, and the left foot in groin of right thigh as shown in Illustration 21. This is the Head Stand in the Lotus Posture. This should be held for a few seconds, to start with, but the time may be increased with practice. To discontinue posture return to original position in easy stages.

At the start this posture may be practiced by a wall or corner of the room so that the wall or walls will serve as additional supports for the body, or it may be performed with the help of another person.

Discretion must be exercised as to how long the posture is held. People whose blood vessels are healthy may hold the inverted position for longer periods.

This exercise should only be learned under a teacher's supervision. Otherwise hemmorrhage may be the sad result due to the condition of the blood vessels of the brain or the eyes (when blood clots will form in the eyes). I have always advised my students not to start this posture until after I have seen them and determined their physical condition.

While in this posture concentrate on the space between the eyebrows.

Benefits:

A huge quantity of blood is sent to the upper regions of body and all organs which normally do not receive that much blood are vitalized. The heart is rested since the flow of venous blood which normally has to be pumped up by the heart against the force of gravity is now aided by it. It is especially useful for those who have much mental work to do.

Parts of the body which usually carry the body's weight are rested, while those which are generally free from weight are exercised. For example, the lower part of the spine is rested while the upper part of the spine and the neck which are now carrying the body's weight are exercised.

The digestive and eliminative systems are also beneficially affected.

The contents of the stomach and intestines press downwards due to the gravitational pull, and these organs have to work hard to keep the contents back in their normal position. This develops the internal muscles. The footlock further rests the heart and increases blood supply to the trunk and brain, and it tones up the whole nervous system.

This posture should be practiced by children. Their brains grow larger, as they grow older, and the process is aided and harmonized by this exercise.

Poor circulation to the brain is often the cause of a lack of balance, neurasthenia, depression, hysteria and other nervous disorders.

Even my students of eighty and more derived benefits from this *āsana*. This is the posture for those who wish to develop suprasensory powers like telepathic communication and clairvoyance.

xx. HEAD STAND IN THE LOTUS POSTURE (VARIATION)

Purpose:

This posture intensifies benefits of the Head Stand in the Lotus Posture *(Sirshāsana)* described in Exercise XIX, p. 90.

Technique:

(Illustration 21). While standing on the head as in Exercise XIX, lower legs slowly until knees are pointing to the floor as shown in Illustration 21. To discontinue posture, allow knees to resume original position and return them to floor as in Exercise XIX.

Illustration 21.   Head Stand in the Lotus Posture

Illustration 21.   (Variation)   Head Stand in the Lotus Posture

XXI. *VAKRĀSANA:*
THE FULL SPINE TWIST

Purpose:

1) To intensify benefits of *Ardha-Vakrāsana* II, the Half Spinal Twist
II, described in Exercise XIV.

2) To vitalize ascending and descending colons (Figure 3, p. 130)
and organs of the lower part of abdomen.

Technique:

(Illustration 22). Place left foot in the right groin with knee on the
floor and right foot on left side of the left knee as shown in Illustration
22. Catch hold of the left knee with the left hand. Place right hand
behind back with fingers touching the right thigh. Rotate body and
head to right side and concentrate on the nape of the neck.

Repeat exercise by reversing position of the legs and rotating body
to left.

Benefits:

It tones up nervous and gastro-intestinal systems and helps to align
vertebrae in natural position. The practitioner develops a firm will,
self-confidence and a feeling of perseverance.

Illustration 22. *Vakrāsana:*
The Full Spine Twist

XXII. *KURMĀSANA I:*
HALF TORTOISE POSTURE

Purpose:

To awaken latent faculties of the mind and body.

Technique..

(Illustration 23). The practitioner should have personal instructions from his teacher before attempting this exercise.

First sit down in the Lotus Posture (*Padmāsana,* Exercise XIII, p. 74) and then insert arms through legs as shown in Illustration 23. Keep the body perfectly balanced while grasping neck with both hands and concentrate on space between eyebrows while breathing normally. *Kurma* means "tortoise" in Sanscrit.

Benefits:

This exercise is one of those which brings radiant health.

Illustration 23. *Kurmāsana I:* Half Tortoise Posture

XXIII. *KURMĀSANA II:*
THE TORTOISE POSTURE

Purpose:

1) To tone up entire body.
2) To relax it.

Technique:

(Illustration 24). Sit down with both legs stretched on the floor and bend forward completely as in Exercise XVIII, p. 88. Place right foot on nape of neck and left foot on ankle of right leg. Fix hands firmly on the floor and balance the body's weight on arms as shown in Illustration 24, and concentrate on the breathing. To discontinue posture, bend arms from elbows slowly and let body descend to the floor. Unfold legs and stretch them.

Benefits:

The benefits of this posture cannot be adequately described. It expands the chest box and increases breathing capacity. It makes the whole body elastic and nimble and prevents ossification of the bones. It corrects flatulence, constipation and other digestive disorders and rejuvenates the entire system.

Illustration 24. *Kurmāsana II:* The Tortoise Posture

xxiv. POSTURE FOR STRETCHING THE THIGHS

Purpose:

1) To stretch pelvic muscles and the tissues which connect the generative organs to thighs.
2) To relieve tension in elbows, pelvic region and muscles of inner thighs.

Technique:

(Illustration 25). Stand with feet about a yard apart, one in front of the other. Now slowly move legs farther apart lowering the torso to the floor. In case strain is felt, resume the standing position. Practice stretching the legs in this way, till the daily stretching of the muscles renders them elastic enough to sit down on the floor. In this posture, concentrate on the breathing.

Benefits:

It tones up the pelvis, legs and sex organs, and relaxes the entire body.

Illustration 25. Posture for Stretching the Thighs

xxv. *HALĀSANA II:*
THE PLOUGH POSTURE II

Purpose:

1) To increase benefits of the Plough Posture I described in Exercise XVI, Page 83.
2) To eliminate excess fat from the abdomen.
3) To tone up the spine.

Technique:

(Illustrations 26 and 26a). Lie on the floor on back with hands stretched on either side of the body. Breathe in and raise legs up all the way, keeping hands on the floor, until the feet touch the floor across the head. Now raise knees slowly and place them on either side of the head with the shanks on the floor as shown in Illustration 26. Concentrate on the nape of the neck.

Benefits:

It increases benefits of Plough Posture I, strengthens spine, increases appetite and reduces accumulation of fat in the abdomen and hips.

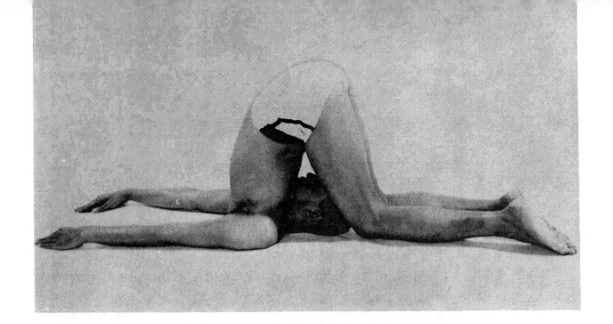

Illustration 26. *Halāsana II:* The Plough Posture II

Illustration 26a. *Halāsana III:* The Plough Posture III

111

XXVI. *BADDHA-PADMĀSANA:*
THE LOCKED LOTUS POSTURE

Purpose:

1) To stretch the chest.
2) To intensify benefits of Lotus Posture *(Padmāsana),* Exercise XIII, p. 74.

Technique:

(Illustration 27). Sit down on a folded blanket and place right foot in left groin, and left foot in right groin. Keep both knees pressed down on the blanket. By passing arms behind the back, grasp toes on right foot with right hand, and those on the left foot with left hand, as shown in Illustration 27.

Benefits:

This posture gives mental and physical balance and soothes the nervous system. It is excellent for meditation and the breathing exercises. The different types of breathing in this posture confer different benefits. Granting perfect equilibrium it releases the practitioner from the pains and miseries of everyday life. Keeping the spine straight it elevates people from their ordinary consciousness, as a lotus is floated by water, into a superconscious state. Because of consciousness of the spine which acts as a tie to the soul, always pulling it down, one is always reminded of body consciousness and we are unable to enter the superconscious or subconscious levels of the mind. But in this posture the superconscious and subconscious are readily entered.

In this posture one controls and retains the outgoing creative and positive forces of the body. It increases appetite and quickens the awakening of the serpent power *kundalini* described in Chapter 4.

112

Illustration 27.   *Baddha-Padmāsana:* The Locked Lotus Posture

XXVII. *SIDDHĀSANA*
THE AUSPICIOUS POSTURE

Technique:

(Illustration 28). Sit on the floor and stretch legs forward. Bend left leg at the knee and press left heel against perineum (the space between anus and the scrotum). Then bend right leg and place heel just above the genitals.

Benefits:

Many yogis and adepts have gained self-realization through meditation in this posture and therefore it is known as the Auspicious Posture. It is an excellent posture for breathing exercises. It engenders virility and moral well-being.

While meditating, the palms of the hands should be placed one on top of the other over the right heel, or the arms may be stretched straight so that the back of right hand is on right knee with fingers touching floor, and the back of left hand is on the left knee with the fingers touching the floor.

Illustration 28. *Siddhāsana:*
The Auspicious Posture

XXVIII. *PĀSINI-ĀSANA:*
THE NOOSE POSTURE

Purpose:

1) To awaken dormant faculties of the mind and body.
2) To eliminate tension.
3) To maintain equilibrium of nervous force in the body.

Technique:

(Illustration 29). Lie on a folded blanket. Bend right leg and passing it under right armpit, place foot on the nape of the neck. Similarly place left leg under left armpit and place foot behind the head as shown in Illustration 29. Stretch arms on either side of the body and concentrate on the navel (solar plexus) while breathing. With each breath in draw up the energy from the solar plexus to the brain and with each breath out bring it down to the solar plexus. The exercise is named after the Sanscrit *Pāsa*, a noose.

Benefits:

This is an excellent posture for achieving self-realization. It brings about better control of the body and mind and improves concentration. It, therefore, contributes to material success.

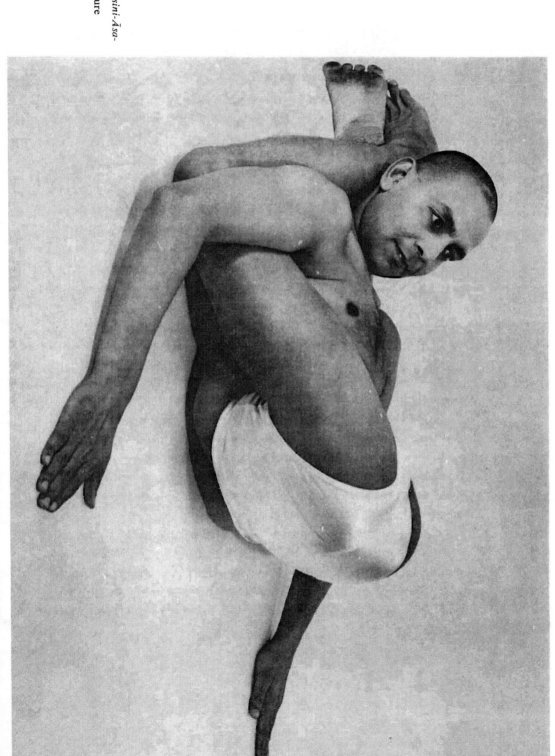

Illustration 29. *Pāśini-Āsa-na:* The Noose Posture

Part Three

13. BREATHING AND

MEDITATION

Until Maynow in the seventeenth century proved otherwise, it was the opinion of European physiologists that the purpose of "breathing" was to "cool the heart." Through his experiments, not only did this British chemist and physiologist prove that breathing was part of the process of excretion (expelling nitrogen and carbon dioxide from the lungs) but that the human body lived not on air, but on a "more active and subtle part of it." He called this *spiritus igneo-aereus*. Maynow was scoffed at until the experiments of Priestley and Lavoisier a century later proved that Maynow's *spiritus igneo-aereus* was "oxygen."

Maynow's "more active and subtle part" of air is only partially accounted for by the hypothesis of "oxygen." Just because we are told we cannot live without oxygen (the yogis *have* for long periods as we have seen in Chapter 4) it does not mean this gas is the activating agent, and not a *more subtle force* (like electricity) of which oxygen is but one of its many manifestations or materializations. This subtle force, this all-permeating force, is what the ancients of more than two thousand five hundred years ago called *prāna* or Cosmic Energy.

According to the Indians the substance of the universe is *ākāsa* (ether) which is "so subtle that it is beyond all ordinary perception; it can only be seen when it has become gross and has taken a form." (Swami Vivekananda in *Rāja Yoga*). This substance of the universe, *ākāsa,* (ether) is activated by the all-pervasive *prāna* (cosmic energy, electricity) to make the universe and man.

The texts say it is the sum total of all the forces existing in the universe. It manifests itself as motion, gravitation, electricity, nerve currents, thought. It is *prāna* through which we hear, it is *prāna* through which the eyes see, the tongue tastes, the nose smells, the skin feels and the intellect functions. The power of music, the impressive words

118

of an orator, the smile on the face of a young girl are all manifestations of *prāna*. It is *prāna* that makes the fire to burn, that makes the wind to blow, the river to flow, the steam engine to work, the jet planes to fly, trains and motors to speed by, the radio waves to travel. It is magnetism, force, "electron" (the microcosm of the macrocosm) and electricity. Without it the blood will not be pumped by the heart or the food digested and assimilated or excreted.

It is *prāna* which makes the lungs to function. It is the power which controls the muscles of the lungs which controls breathing. So the yogis discovered that by controlling breathing they could control *prāna*, the life giving energy, and therefore life itself and all its activities. Although there are ten forms of pranic energy described in our ancient texts like *apana* that excretes, *samana* that digests, *krikara* that produces hunger and thirst (and there are methods of yoga for controlling all) it is the pranic energy which motivates breathing that may be most readily controlled, and through it the others. That is why yogis practice *prānāyāma* which literally means "breathpause," (in Sanscrit *prāna* "breath," *āyāma* "pause").

Every human breathes about 21,000 times a day or about 15 times a minute. It is the theory of yoga that each person has been allotted a definite number of breaths to his life. If he uses these up rapidly by quick breathing he will die sooner. So the yogi tries to regulate and slow his breath down (and even to the extent of stopping breathing for long periods).

As soon as *prāna* has been controlled, all the other actions of *prāna* in the body will slowly come under control and, consequently, one achieves control of each voluntary and involuntary organ in the body. Furthermore, the yogi will be able through concentration to send *prāna* to any part of his body which he may wish to develop. He may direct it to his solar plexus to make it function more efficiently as an "abdominal brain." In the animal kingdom we have examples of perceptions which we do not possess. For instance, animals can see in the dark and they hear sounds which are inaudible to humans. Through the direction of *prāna* to the appropriate organs the yogi recaptures all these powers. In the animal world it is the correct use of *prāna* which has resulted in the particular configuration of each an-

119

imal. Because he needed a long neck to reach the leaf-fodder on tall trees, the giraffe grew a long neck through centuries of evolution by sending more *prāṇā* to his neck. Through a similar process the rabbit has long ears, the elephant a long trunk, *homo sapiens* a larger brain than the Neanderthaler, and the physical culturalist a taller figure or bigger biceps since, through concentration, he has sent more *prāṇā* to the spine or the biceps. However, in general, it is true that, today, people have lost control of even the use of simple muscles, through lack of proper *prāṇā* transmission to them.

Bodily or mental diseases are due to the unbalanced condition of *prāṇā* in the organism. When it does not travel freely to the digestive organs we get indigestion. When it does not travel freely to organs of elimination, the body gets poisoned. But *prāṇāyāma* distributes the vital force equally throughout the body. Through its practice surplus vital energy is taken away from certain parts and the parts of the body which are deficient in vital force are supplied with it. Accumulation of *prāṇā* where it is not needed may also create metabolic disharmony or disease. A man with a rich supply of *prāṇā*, who has learned its control through *prāṇāyāma,* is able to transfer it to other people who are unwell and in need of it.

It happens in everyday life that people like to sit and mix with those who are healthy in mind and body and are vital, while they feel uncomfortable if they are in the company of the sick. This, also, is due to the effect of one person's *prāṇā* on another. Times without number I have noticed that during my lectures when I am specially enthusiastic my audience was moved. That was because my speech-vibrations carried to them the extra *prāṇā* that I had summoned to my aid to express my ideas persuasively.

Through the practice of *prāṇāyāma* one *does* actually perceive that the whole world is made of subtle vibrations. Certain drugs and gases like ammonia may also induce this state. Thought is vibration and everything in the universe is vibration. Thoughts are but small whirlpools of vibration and force in the great ocean of universal flux. They are thought whirlpools in a big ocean of thoughts. That is why yogis say that they perceive everything not in physical space *(mahākāsa)* but in mental space *(Chittākāsa).* But the final goal of the highest form of yoga, *Rāja Yoga*, is to perceive everything in "knowledge space" (*chidākāsa*), and *prānāyāma* is the chief instrument through which this is reached. In *Hatha Yoga* too (which is initially meant to keep the body healthy) the breathing exercises are important.

Yoga breathing differs from the Western system in that its aim is not to build a bigger chest but to increase oxygenation of the blood. There are three kinds of breathing known to the West and they all consist of merely inhaling and exhaling. In the first, the upper part of the chest is expanded by taking in air into the upper part of the lungs, the chest is blown out. Too little air is involved in the process. In the second type, which is the intercostal, the middle section of the lungs is employed and somewhat more air is taken in. The third type which is abdominal has become popular in Europe during the last twenty years. In this, air is taken into the lower part of the lungs, and the diaphram is pressed against the abdomen which is thrust out.

But the chief yoga breathing is done in three parts. One first inhales to fill the lower lungs and takes it up to the rib box to expand the thorax and finally one swells out the upper part of the lungs, still inhaling. All this is done as a continuous process in one long inhalation when one has become proficient at it. The exhalation should follow the same pattern, that is, the breath should be expelled first from the lower lungs, then from the thorax and lastly from the upper part. Again, unlike in the West, some yoga breathing is done in three stages, *puraka* (inhalation), *kumbhaka* (retention) and *rechaka* (exhalation).

In general the average student need only know that the purpose of *prānāyāma* is to control the very force of which we are a manifestation and thus control the motions of the mind, the body, the nerves and the glands. When *prānā* is distributed evenly through the body we achieve psycho-physical co-ordination and get rid of our emotional complexes and are free of the thraldom of the mental unbalance which gives rise to fear, anger, envy, or a sense of inferiority.

It is also the purpose of yoga breathing not to dissipate the cosmic energy that we have in our breaths. Breath and pranic energy is lost with every activity. So the yogi retains and directs it to particular centers through *prānāyāma*. Each and every cell in the blood which daily travels through the body must be charged with *prānā*. All the astral tubes or *nādis* which are known to yoga must be flushed with *prāna* so that every organ gets its proper share and is stimulated to carry on its proper function. We shall have more to say about the *nādi-s* in the chapter on *The Control of Psychic Forces* (See Chapter 13).

Before attempting *pranāyāma* one should learn some preparatory breathing like Cleansing Breathing, Positive Breathing and Breathing to Calm the Mind. After practicing these breathing exercises one should find oneself ready to learn *pranāyāma.*Generally my students take about two weeks to learn the preliminary exercises. The techniques of *prānāyāma* could be learned in a week's time, but it takes months to attain perfection in its practice.

I. CLEANSING BREATHING

Technique:

This exercise may be practiced while standing or while sitting on a chair, or on the floor. Before starting the exercise, clean the nostrils thoroughly by blowing them hard.

Now close the right nostril with the right index finger and breathe in quickly through the left nostril. As soon as the breath is full, remove pressure from the right nostril and close left nostril with the left index finger. Breathe out completely through the right nostril. There should be no retention of breath and the inhaling and exhaling should be done in quick succession. To start with twelve such breaths should be taken, but with practice, they may be increased to fifty.

Benefits:

This exercise purifies the blood, strengthens the nerves and even tones up the nostrils themselves. Just as overseers and engineers construct new highways and byways in the forest for an army to march, similarly this "cleansing breath" paves a clean, smooth path for the student of yoga to master *prānāyāma* (Exercise IV) and other forms of yoga breathing.

II. POSITIVE BREATHING

Technique:

As in previous exercise, the posture for Positive Breathing may be any

122

convenient one like standing up or sitting down on a chair or on the floor, but care should be taken that the spine and head are straight, the shoulders are dropped, and that no part of the body is moved while breathing.

Close left nostril with right ring finger (fourth finger of right hand) and take a deep breath through the right nostril for the count of eight or eight heart-beats. Now close both nostrils with the right thumb and right ring finger. Retain breath for six heart-beats.

Now relieve pressure from right nostril and keeping left nostril closed, breathe out through the right nostril for eight heart-beats. Repeat the exercise five times to begin with and, with practice, increase it to fifteen times. Do not produce unnecessary sound while inhaling and exhaling, or distort the muscles of the face.

Benefits:

This exercise balances the positive and negative currents which control our entire body. We should practice it when we feel negative. After leaving the company of people whom we have found negative, and the negative forces we have absorbed in their company cannot be gotten rid of (their store of *prāna* being low) this exercise should be practiced in a well ventilated room, in an open park, or on the roof of one's house. Positive Breathing strengthens the nerves and makes them steady.

III. BREATHING TO CALM THE MIND

Technique:

This exercise may be performed while standing, sitting on a chair or on the floor, or while lying on the floor, or on a hard bed. Keep the spine straight with hands on either side of the body.

Concentrating on the breath, take a deep breath through both nostrils for the count of eight or for eight heart-beats. Retain breath for two to four heart-beats. Now exhale for eight heart-beats concentrating all the time on the breath.

Benefits:

Practice this breathing when disturbed by emotions like anger or disgust. I have seen my students look serene and calm after regular practice of Breathing to Calm the Mind.

IV. *PRĀNĀYĀMA*

This is one of the simple exercises of *prānāyāma* which may be practiced without the guidance of a teacher. It should be attempted after practicing the first three breathing exercises for at least two weeks, ten to fifteen minutes every day.

Technique:

Close right nostril with right thumb and fill the lungs with a slow, steady breath, counting six, and concentrating the mind on the *Idā* (the left nerve current which travels through the spine along the left *nādi* from the left nostril to the root of the spinal cord, Figure 1, p. 23). Visualize that the nerve currents are being sent down with the breath along the *Idā* to the last plexus of the spine, the *Mulādhāra Lotus,* or the seat of the kundalini force (Figure 1). Hold the current there for the count of four. Now close left nostril with the right ring finger and exhale through the right nostril visualizing that the nerve current is being slowly drawn upwards with the breath through the *Pingalā* (the right *nādi* which carries the nerve current from the last plexus to the right nostril, Figure 1). Do this for six counts.

Now reverse the procedure.

This makes one *prānāyāma*. Practice three to begin with, increase it to six, and then to twelve.

V. CONCENTRATION *(DHĀRANA)*

There are four steps involved in controlling the mind:

1) *Pratyāhāra* or introspection for controlling the senses.
2) *Dhārana* or concentration.
3) *Dhyāna* or meditation.
4) *Samādhi* or achieving a state of supreme peace.

The *chittā* or mind-stuff is in a continual state of flux and is ever restless. It is an ocean of sense impressions, ideas, emotions, decisions, memories and such volitions of the ego as "I" and "You." The mind going out through the senses is chaotic and tends to dissipate itself. It

124

must therefore be first ingathered and steadied through *pratyāhāra* or introspection. The steadied mind is then given a singleness of purpose through *dhārana* or concentration by fixing it on a single object like a rose or the tip of a candle flame. Through concentration we achieve meditation or *dhyāna*. Through tranquil meditation and the utter absorption of mind-stuff and cosmic energy *(chittā* and *pranā)* in the entire organism ("the dissolution of the mind in the self") not only is physical balance and well-being reached, but the state of *samādhi* or "the peace that passeth all understanding."

Among the manifold distractions of the Western world people find it difficult to concentrate and achieve singleness of purpose. There have been great men in the West, of course, whose genius and singleness of purpose elevated them above all men. But they were the exceptions rather that the rule and, I think, people who have been to India and found it a land of spirituality and devotion to ideals will agree with me that the Indians tend to develop concentration and singleness of purpose more easily. I am not claiming any superior virtues for India. I am merely suggesting that the age-old systems of metaphysics and mind-control have made it easier for many Indians to understand the nature of reality and control of the self, and that in this age of East-West cultural and material exchange, India has this to give: the achievement of psychophysical well-being through the banishing of distractions and the concentration of mental and physical forces through yoga. The East and West have bountifully contributed to the progress of mankind. Now the time seems ripe when they should more readily pool their knowledge for mutual benefit. This little book is offered to the West and especially to America (where I now reside) in that spirit.

To return to the subject of concentration, I have found that, in India, students like to concentrate on a picture of the Lord or of that of their *guru,* but that in America they prefer to concentrate on the extremity of the nose or the tip of a burning candle. To make it easier for such people I have suggested to them that they may concentrate on any object or picture of their choice.

Concentrate until the mind is well absorbed with the object of concentration. It helps to calm down the emotions and it clarifies ideas.

125

It will help in material progress too since the output and quality of work improves.

When concentrating on an object do not fight with the mind. All strain on mind and body should be avoided. Ignore disturbing emotions and they will soon pass away.

But do not attempt concentration while hungry or in some acute pain. When concentration is attempted on the flame of a candle, the eyes should be half closed and the gaze fixed on the upper part of the flame. One should either stand, or sit on the floor, or on a chair, and place the burning candle on a table about six to ten feet away, with the flame on a level with the eyes.

When concentration has been achieved for twelve seconds without closing the eyes, one is ready for meditation.

VI. SAMĀDHI:
PERFECT BLISS

After mastering the art of concentration, one proceeds to meditate. The constant practice of meditation leads to realization of self.

The sight of an apple on a table makes one know that an apple is there. But there are many vital parts of the brain, spine and other parts of the body of which we are not conscious. Yoga brings all these to a person's consciousness. Yoga is really the study of "you."

Many actions of the body are done consciously, while others are done unconsciously. For instance we eat food consciously. But after that the actions of digestion, assimilation and most aspects of elimination are done unconsciously. We cannot stop these processes. Similarly we cannot stop the heart-beat or the workings of the lungs, unless we have become conscious of them, and are able to control them through yoga. All the voluntary and involuntary actions of the body are done by "you" and you alone. There are not many actions in the body which can work independently of your will if you are exerting yogic control. It is when you have risen into this state, above ordinary body consciousness, and are able to control it, that you are in the state of samādhi.

Samādhi may be likened to sleep when we become conscious of certain workings of our subconscious mind. But when a yogi enters into

126

"sleep" the benefits he receives are different. *Samādhi* is different from the subconscious state. It is the superconscious state. Unlike in sleep, it is the conscious realization of the workings of the unconscious. It is beyond reason.

Reason is limited. One cannot prove through work-a-day reasoning that the soul is immortal, that one is without birth or death, or that one is beyond the reach of misery, suffering and pain. The normal human mind has shown its inability to prove these things. But these are important factors whicn govern human life. They should be realized through yoga meditation. Yoga teaches transcendent reason. By degrees it teaches us the way to transcend the mind. Instinct develops into reason and reason into transcendental consciousness.

Yogis and prophets who attained this superconscious knowledge were ordinary men like you and me. And every man has the right to reach perfection and knowledge. Reaching of this superconscious state is true religion.

VII. DIFFERENCE BETWEEN CONCENTRATION AND *SAMĀDHI*

Concentration is the fixation of the mind on a certain internal or external object. When the mind has been trained on a particular object and it continuously keeps it in the mind-flow (as in a continuous stream of electricity) that is good concentration.

In meditation one visualizes the object of concentration, for instance a candle flame, with some intensity. When one sees the light of the candle in the chamber of the heart or in the mind for a longer period with the same intensity, that is meditation. When one can meditate continuously on the internal perception of which the object was merely the cause, that is *samādhi*.

When the mind has succeeded by concentration in perceiving the external courses of sensations, by themselves, such as sound which is due to vibrations outside, the mind acquires the ability to perceive all material existence. When it succeeds in perceiving these motions within itself during meditation then it has complete control of itself. These perceived motions are merely the results of the nerve currents which have carried external vibrations or the external currents to the mind.

127

When one has succeeded in perceiving the mental reactions by themselves (which were caused when the external vibrations carried by nerve motion to the mind were reacted upon by the mind to impart knowledge of objects) one knows everything, since every material object that may be perceived is only perceived in a similar manner. Then only does one acquire miraculous *siddhi-s,* those powers like telepathy, levitation or the materialization of any physical object. These should not be used as an end in themselves. The rationale of materializing objects which is beyond ordinary comprehension is because in *samādhi* the Yogi has become identified with the Primal Force. Identified with light and part of the final reality of cosmos, at least the furthest reality we can ever reach, the yogi (should he so wish) is no longer subject to the law of gravitation. He no longer has any "weight" like other material objects. His mind, released from his gross, his corporeal self, is free to roam the universe. It is part of the Primal Stuff *which it may affect at will.* He has attained an extraordinary state, gotten behind the veil of *Maya* (Appearance) to the only true and effective constantly creating and destroying reality that is the eternal flux, the Primal Force. As Primal Force he is beyond all delusions like matter and its gravitation weight, or the concepts of space and time. As Primal Force, which is all pervasive, he is one with the light that is an atom, or water, or land, or a planet. He travels with ease over the light rays that are water or land or air. And as Primal Force, the yogi may affect the architecture of the conglomerations of light atoms (which is all matter) to satisfy a personal wish or that of a supplicant.

It is only when one has, through meditation, identified himself with the Primal Force and this Idea, that one becomes a full fledged yogi radiating peace, joy, bliss and happiness. Then only will you know your true self. This is true religion. Yoga is not a religion in itself, but when practiced it leads to self-knowledge or to religion. Persons with religion or without (atheists) may all practice yoga as the study of their own selves and through their own experiences come to their own conclusions. In my opinion this is the best way. Whether they want to practice a particular religion or not, it will never retard their growth in the path of self-study and self-discipline.

VIII. CONTROL OF PSYCHIC FORCES

The rhythmic breathing of yoga creates nerve-currents in the body of the practitioner. There are two chief nerve-currents in the spinal column, as we have already seen, the positive and the negative, one of which carries the currents to the brain and the other from the brain to the last nerve plexus of the spine. The various types of yoga breathing help in controlling the various nerve centers of the body as well as the seven nerve plexuses or seven lotuses of the spinal cord (Figure 3, p. 130).

By yoga breathing alone one may control the motion of the lungs and other involuntary movements, as well as the more subtle movements like sight and hearing.

Proportion of inhalation, retention and exhalation having been learned under the able guidance of a teacher, the breathing harmonizes the system and confers benefits which are too innumerable to mention. To give a simple example, after the first week of yoga breathing, wrinkles disappear from the face, there is a wonderful improvement to the voice (one can never find a yogi with a harsh voice) and since the nerves and the mind have been calmed, there is a constant expression of calmness on the face.

By constant practice of yoga breathing the serpent power *kundalini* at the base of the spine (*mulādhāra* lotus) is aroused and is made to travel up the spine through the other plexuses to the greatest nerve center in the medulla known as *Sahasrāra* lotus, the Abode of Bliss. It is not part of the brain but floats independently in the cerebral fluid. In other words the nerve plexus *Sahasrāra* may be compared to a lotus and the spinal column to its stalk. Just as a lotus floats on the water with its roots in the river bed below, so does this lotus float in the cerebral fluid with its roots down below in the last nerve plexus, the *mulādhāra*.

Through yoga breathing the positive and negative nerve-currents that pass along the *Idā* and *Pingalā* on either side of the spinal cord are brought under control. They no longer pass along these channels but travel through the central channel called *sushumnā* which has now been opened up through the breathing exercises. In all living

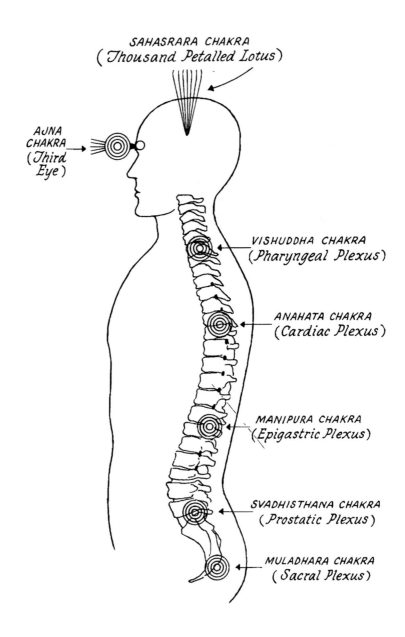

Figure 3. *Chakras,* or Nerve Centers

130

beings with a spinal column, this channel is normally closed. As the nerve currents rise to reach the *sahasrāra* center, the different nerve centers of the spine are opened, consequently opening, one by one, different layers of the mind, leading the practitioner beyond senses, and beyond the intellect where reasoning power can never reach. This state is the superconscious state. It is in this state that psychic forces may be controlled.

Part Four

14. THE NECESSITY FOR

YOGA IN THE MODERN WORLD

I have often been asked what is the point of practicing yoga breathing in a place like New York where the air is saturated with gasoline fumes, smoke and soot from the chimneys of factories. It is more necessary to practice yoga breathing in a place like New York than it is in a seaside or hill health resort. Everybody needs a certain amount of oxygen to purify his blood every day. In the open air, on the seashore, riverside, or forest or mountains (so long as they are not very high) one gets enough oxygen with less effort and with fewer breaths, while in a city like New York one has to practice scientific breathing regularly to get the necessary supply. Normal people cannot stop breathing, and one cannot postpone breathing until one returns to the country or to the suburbs!

With my American students I have noticed that after the practice of yoga, they are never fatigued and their feeling of disinterestedness in their work has vanished.

I have known instances when a yogi swallowed a test tube full of cholera germs before a gaping audience. The fact that a test tube of cholera germs (sufficient to kill off an entire regiment) could do no harm was due to the power of concentration and of resistance to germs and disease that the yogi had built up through the practice of his science. Prevention is better than cure. I have also known yogis who swallowed acids or arsenic without any harmful effects. Furthermore I have been in this country for three years without a single physical ailment.

One should try to restore one's health while remaining in one's normal place of residence and continuing one's work. One does not achieve a healthy body merely by fleeing to the Himalayas, California, Florida or other health resorts. Health must be earned, earned through daily practice of the exercises I have described in this book. It cannot be bought.

The yoga system of exercising bestows benefits which are somewhat different to those which are supposed to accrue to one through the Western systems of physical culture or through the popular sports.

15.   THE NECESSITY FOR

A TEACHER

The relationship between teacher and student in Yoga is a very close one, and is not entered into lightly. In India, a teacher will not accept as pupil everyone who wishes to study under him, but chooses his students carefully after satisfying himself that they are qualified to receive the full Yogic teachings. Consequently this book which is intended for the general reader has been confined to that part of yoga which may be transmitted through the written word. It is the same with the Indian texts on yoga. They are meant as the skeletons of yoga technique to which the flesh is added through the personal guidance and care of a teacher.

It is not always necessary for students to stay with their teacher as they do in India. A student may have his lessons from the teacher and practice at home. In India, students have great faith in their teacher and devotion towards him. Living near the teacher has great advantages, especially when one tries to transmit the power of *kundalini* from one nerve center to another, or one is attempting to get the full benefits of the exercises.

At the *ashram* where I first learned yoga I sought the company of my teacher at least twice a day. He would offer me a seat but I preferred to sit at his feet to receive the benefits of his spiritual aura. I used to lay bare to him the secrets of my heart and have his sympathy and guidance and, afterwards I used to emerge into the open air with a feeling of success, full of strength and courage to fight the obstructions on my personal path of evolution. There are many difficulties which arise during the practice of yoga which may only be solved by a teacher.

Especially when one practices meditation, the guidance of a teacher is necessary. There are many obstacles in the way. The mere presence of my teacher was inspiring to me. His very company was self-illumination. Until I lived with him I never believed that a teacher could take away *karma-s* (fruits of past deeds) from a student into his own keeping, or that he could awaken the *kundalini* in a student through mere sight, touch or words. A teacher transmits spirituality to students just as easily as if he were handing over a book.

Some people say that a teacher is not necessary for learning yoga. A teacher is indispensable. Just as an instructor is necessary for learning to drive a car, or to learn medicine, so is an instructor necessary for learning the science of yoga. Just as a hen hatches its eggs by sitting on them, or fishes and tortoises in the ocean hatch their eggs by looking at them, (as our ancients have said) so can a teacher transmit spiritual power through touch, sight or thought. Sometimes it happens that a teacher will ask his student sitting before him to close his eyes and then he will transmit his spiritual power to him.

Those students who are only interested in the improvement of their mental and physical health need not devote much time in the company of the teacher. Generally I advise my students to have ten to fifteen sessions with me and after that to correspond with me if they encounter any difficulties. But those students who really want to develop higher faculties and powers in themselves need more perseverance and should be with their teacher for several years.

16. FOOD AND HEALTH

In ancient times (and even today in certain parts of India where seclusion was sought to practice the higher forms of yoga) people lived mostly on fruits, vegetables and root vegetables. They were as far as possible uncooked.

Although I am myself a vegetarian, I do not criticize people for being non-vegetarian, either partially or wholly. However, I do emphasize that it is important to eat in moderation whether one is vegetarian or not. People imagine that as soon as we have finished eating, the job is over and done with. On the other hand the ancient system of Indian medicine, *Ayurveda,* which is more than three thousand years old, says it takes more than a month for the food to be completely digested and assimilated. According to the ancients it takes that much time for the food to get assimilated into the seven different components of the body which are: 1) chyle, 2) blood, 3) flesh, 4) fat, 5) bone, 6) marrow, 7) sperm.

In each of these components resides its characteristic "fire" or energy with the help of which food is refined and the gross matter separated from the fine matter. Within twenty-four hours of eating, the roughage like cellulose and other wastes leave the body with the help of the bowels and intestines and the finer part becomes one with the chyle *(rasa).* With the aid of the energy in chyle the food elements in it are separated into waste known as phlegm (*shlesman,* which sounds very much like "phlegm") and the finer part becomes one with the blood. With the help of the "fire in the blood, food is once more separated into two elements one of which is bile, which is hot and firey, wet and acrid, and the other part becomes one with flesh. It is bile which extracts the energies of food in the stomach and, in fact, the intestinal fire residing in the stomach is bile. Again, due to the "fire" in the flesh, the food in it is separated, in a similar manner, into fat and into waste products, such as ear wax, and the fat in its turn changes the food elements in it to bone and perspiration. Then the energy in the bone sends out waste matter in the form of nails and hair and the fine part of the food becomes one with marrow. The food element in the marrow, with the help of the "fire" residing there, in its turn becomes the red cells in blood, and sperm, and the gross elements, waste products such as eye secretions. The sperm is pure and does not contain any waste. Through the yoga system its energy may be transmuted to awaken the force *kundalini*.

I have related all this to show that the ancients considered assimilation to be a very complicated process which took a period of many days. It is impressive that the ancients knew that it is the combustion that takes place in the blood cells that provides new cells, and that the cells excrete waste products (like carbon dioxide, excess water and the gross part from protein metabolism); and that fat represents reserve fuel for new cells. Although blood circulation was not discovered until 1628 by William Harvey of Britain, the ancients not only understood it and controlled it through various yoga exercises, but long before Galvani (who said that electricity is generated in the muscles) they knew of the electrical impulses that motivate the body and quite rightly saw their connection with light and other phenomena.

I am in favor of vegetarianism not because animals, birds and fishes have to be killed to be eaten, but because vegetarian food contains all the things the body needs and it is more nourishing than flesh. According to the ancients the human body is made of five elements: air, earth, water, fire and ether. All these elements are present in their most nutrient form in vegetables and fruits. Those who eat meat or fish or dairy products (eggs, milk and cheese) do not get their nutrition directly from the best source as many animals do, but indirectly from the bodies of animals. It is for this reason that I prefer vegetarian food as the best for maintaining the body's health.

Those who practice yoga need less food. They are able to extract the five elements directly from the atmosphere itself as the plants do. All fruit, nuts, grains and vegetables are nothing but these elements — air, earth, fire, water and ether — compounded into food by the rays of the sun. Therefore, the best way to get these elements is from the atmosphere itself through breathing and sun baths. The second best way is to have them from the fruits and vegetables, and the third, to absorb them from the dairy products. Milk and eggs are less gross than flesh.

To yoga and *ayurveda* all things like animals, birds, fishes, vegetables, human beings and apparently inert matter like a piece of rock, are made of the same element pervaded with force. The force manifested in man has made him one of the superior beings of creation, but that same life force resides in a piece of rock in an unmanifested condition. The difference is one of degree, not of kind.

Not only is there physical unity among us all since we are made of the same matter, but our very thoughts are of the same substance. There is a complete similarity between your thought and mine. When your thought enters my head the two thoughts are the same and have the same configuration and vibrations. All thoughts come from the one great ocean of thought.

The more we extend this outlook, the nearer do we approach the true reality. If we generalized the term "human beings" we would perceive that all human beings are the same. Extending that idea we would soon see that men and animals are the same. Carrying this idea still further we realize that plants and animals and even apparently lifeless matter like the metal uranium are the same.

According to yoga belief, one needs food, not for energy, but for the building materials it brings. The yogis believe energy does not come from food. If food were energy, people would never sleep but would merely work and eat continuously. It is only *prānā,* the all pervasive or primal force, which is energy. This is absorbed when the individual unites with the Universal unconsciously during sleep, or consciously during samādhi. The human body made up of the five elements (air, earth, fire, water, ether) needs these materials from food as building material. These elements are found more in vegetables than in dairy products only because the plants utilize these elements directly, while most animals get them at second hand from the vegetable world. Vegetables which are grown in the sun and in fresh air and on organic soil where chemicals have not been used, are especially rich in the five elements.

One needs very little food if the food is of the right type, as Mahatma Gandhi so ably showed the world. Even his many fasts merely rejuvenated his body since he was very intelligently resting his organs of digestion and assimilation.

138

When food is over-cooked, much of the nutritive value in it is dissipated into the air and part of the disintegration which should have taken place in the stomach takes place outside. The appetizing smells of cooking foods represent values that have been released and wasted in the air. These should properly have been made available to the body. How do we know that the most essential and subtle part of food has not been wasted by cooking? When food that has not been deprived of its subtle life-giving elements in this manner is eaten, very little of it will suffice to thoroughly motorize the mind and body.

I have myself lived on uncooked fruits and vegetables for more than twenty years and feel much better for it.

However, it is not advisable for anyone to change suddenly from a non-vegetarian diet. People would be well advised to make the transition gradually.

I recommend heartily the use of sprouted grains, nuts and other seeds. Sprouted grains contain special nutritive qualities not present in the dormant grain, and serve to round out a fruit and vegetable diet. I myself lived completely on sprouted grain for six months. It may be prepared in your apartment or even in a hotel room where there is no kitchen, and has the advantage of being very cheap.

When grains start sprouting the starch and proteins are converted into nutrients capable of nourishing the newly born sprout. This is the reason sprouted grain is very beneficial to the aged, the very young, or invalids. Malted milk and biscuits (malt is prepared from germinated barley) are excellent for babies. Those people who cannot stomach a heavy breakfast will find that they will relish a liberal breakfast of sprouted nuts, grains and seeds. The Chinese are very wise in eating great quantities of soya bean sprouts. The traditional Indian and Ceylonese breakfast of *dosa* of which great quantities are eaten are made of the sprouted grain of a leguminous seed called *urad dhall*.

Eating sprouted grain and seeds gives one the same results as an intravenous injection of glucose. The predigested starch and proteins and fats pass readily into the blood stream in the form of sugars and amino-acids. Sprouted food is even better than fruits since fruits begin to lose their nutritive value after they are plucked (in America many fruits are picked before they ripen). On the other hand the sprouted grains are still literally growing on your spoon and they are rich in vitamins and mineral salts. Many nutritive elements that we still know nothing about are created in the process of sprouting.

By eating a liberal quantity of sprouted grain, one need not worry what vitamins are present in the food, and which are lacking.

Sprouted grains are full of good natural taste. The content of fruit sugars is increased by germination. One notices while eating bread that it tastes sweet although the bread has been salted. This happens because the starch has been converted to glucose by the gastric juices. A similar process is continually going on in a germinating seed.

Many grains and seeds like mung beans, lentils, peas, corn, barley, rye, millet, almonds, sesame seed, pistachio, sunflower seeds and peanuts may be sprouted for the table. Red clover seed, radish seed, alfalfa and soybean seed when sprouted are good agents for flavoring as well as nutrition.

Seeds and grains are sprouted by keeping them in water for ten to eighteen hours and then covering them with a damp cloth for twelve to eighteen hours, according to room temperature.

17. SIGNIFICANCE OF COLOR

FOR HEALTH

Although colors play an important part in the maintenance of
health, we seldom pay much attention to them. The color of
the walls in a room, the color of the curtains, the colors of the dresses
and the colors of the fruits and vegetables we eat play an important
part in our life.

We feel the soothing effect of the green of grass and trees in a park or
in the country. We feel the beneficial effect of the vast blue sky or a
lake among the mountains. Colors affect animals, insects and human
beings. That life reacts to color may be proved in this fashion.
Wrap some of the fruit on a tomato plant in white, green and black
cloth. When the other fruits on the plant have ripened remove the
coverings. It will then be seen that the fruit wrapped with green and
white cloth will have ripened, but not those wrapped in black cloth. The
effect of the colors of vegetables on human beings is just as dramatic
and has been emphasized in our ancient medical texts.

They say that some of the most subtle properties of fruits and vegetables are part of their color. This is not surprising to modern scientists who know that it is the orange color in carrots, carotin, that improves vision in the dark. During the last war, the night fighter pilots
were fed with great quantities of carrots. In a similar way, *ayurveda*
says, yellow is necessary for the sacrococcygeal plexus which is situated between the anus and generative organs. It stores this color whenever there is a surplus.

It is a fact that the colors of the spectrum are all due to vibration
of light at different wave-lengths. Violet is the color produced when
waves are short and have a high frequency, while the others, indigo,
blue, green, yellow, orange, red, have progressively longer wave-
lengths, and a progressively lower frequency. On either side of the
visible spectrum there are the invisible ultra-violet or actinic rays, with
a high frequency, and the infra-red or heat waves, with a low frequency.

It, therefore, stands to reason that since we are all but charges of electricity which is manifested in waves and varying frequencies (according to modern science) the various colors which are also waves and frequencies would have a disturbing or beneficial effect on the organism. While food is being broken down for assimilation in the stomach, surely the different types of vibration (which are the different colors) will have their different effects on the various types of vibration that are constantly going on in our bodies to give us human form!

The Indians who had some of the greatest schools of logic the world has ever known, inferred all this, not haphazardly, but from a profound understanding of the atomic structure of matter, and of the one force which animates and preserves this structure (electricity or *prāna*) and which, through disposing itself in various geometric patterns, creates each known element.

About three thousand years ago Kanada who was nicknamed "the eater of atoms" because he thought of food as made up of atoms, expounded the "atomic theory" which became a part of that branch of philosophy known as *vaisheshika* which we described earlier. He declared that atoms made up the universe and that there is unceasing vibratory motion in them. He thought of the atom as a miniature solar system and described the smallest possible unit of time as the time taken by an atom to travel its own length. The other vaisheshika treatises of two thousand five hundred years ago deal with magnets and magnetized needles and their movements towards magnets, the heat of the sun being responsible for the heat in food, firewood and all other substances, the relativity of time and space, the molecular change brought about in substances by heat, the definition of "the atom" as *ayus* or the final, indivisible part of matter, the "cosmic rays" theory where heat and light are conceived as small particles shooting forth in all directions at incredible speed, the circulation of water in plants, the law of gravitation and many other subjects too numerous to mention which are today scientific speculations or facts.

Therefore, I suggest, that we pay heed to the testimony of the ancients, that color has an important bearing on mental and bodily health. They have said that all the colors of the rainbow are present in fruits and vegetables (which they have got from the sun) and that when these colors are ingested into the body, they are stored up in the different plexuses of the body. For instance, white, which represents the water element in the body, is stored in the prostatic plexus situated at the root of the generative organs. Deficiency in white will retard the functions of this plexus. Red is stored in the solar plexus. It represents the sun element. Sufficient red ensures normal working of this plexus. Green, which represents the air element, is stored in the cardiac plexus and it controls the functions of the heart. Blue, which represents ether, is stored in the laryngeal plexus and controls the power of hearing.

Red, which controls the subconscious mind and the primary instincts and desires, also supplies the life force — *prāna*. It develops physical power and strength, courage, love, enthusiasm, leadership, sociableness and generosity. This color may be had in beet, radishes, red cabbage, watercress, spinach, plums, damsons, blackberries, currants and many other berries.

Green influences the heart, blood pressure and the emotions, and vitalizes the nerves. It also imparts wisdom, peace, harmony, sympathy and generosity.

Like green, indigo brings relaxation to the mind. Royal blue and emerald green have a revitalizing effect. Vermilion brings inspiration. Orange strengthens the nerves. A deep vermilion stimulates the body. Moonlight blue brings restfulness to the spirit. Golden rose vitalizes it. Amethyst, purple and violet stimulate the soul.

With the help of these colors in meditation and food, I have seen my students achieve tremendous benefits.

These various colors may be ingested into the body by concentrating on the different nerve plexuses where they are stored. The second best way of absorbing these colors is through fruits and vegetables. Concentration on these plexuses sometimes awakens latent powers and opens the nerve centers for the ascent of the *kundalini* power. It should therefore be practiced under a teacher.

18. RELAXATION

It is a fact that animals and birds know better how to relax than human beings. Relaxation is very important to humans, however, especially in the West, where competition is great, and people live under continual mental, physical and emotional strain. Tension becomes a habit which taxes the muscles, nerves and mind, and results in wasted energy. A few minutes of proper relaxation give the benefit of hours of sleep. Also, many people feel tired when they wake up in the morning because they have not relaxed properly during the night and consequently have used up more energy than they have been producing.

We have impulses and counter-impulses during the day which bring about tension. A man who is irritable by nature is always tense. He is continuously wasting nerve energy and brain power. Although he may be strong in physique, he is sick. In order to enjoy psycho-physiological well-being one should eliminate all feelings of anger, fear or anxiety through the art of relaxation. By relaxing properly during the day, we achieve powers of concentration and restful sleep at night. Relaxation distributes the blood evenly throughout the body, and blood pressure becomes normal.

The pose I prefer for relaxing is shown in Illustration 30 (See also 31) and the following is a guide for doing so: Do not move muscles and limbs. The message of relaxation should be communicated by the mind to the part of the body to be relaxed. Whenever you want to relax a particular part, don't hold it consciously in any one position; just let it rest naturally. One may relax while lying on the bed or on a rug, to start with. Once the art is learned, one may practice relaxation while sitting in a chair or standing in the street. One should let the mind wander through the entire body, fixing it on each part in turn, until one knows that that is perfectly relaxed. The blood rushes to the section on which the mind is concentrated. By thinking of parts of our body, and through sending extra blood and *prāna* there, we should energize and, then, relax these parts. The tensions are all in the different nerve

Illustration 30. Relaxing Posture

Illustration 31. Relaxing Posture

plexuses as the yogis have found out through long concentration and meditation.

In my class in America, I can tell when my students are trying to relax and on exactly which part of their bodies they are concentrating. It takes about two weeks to learn to relax the body and mind completely. At first one should try to relax all the external parts of the body. After that, one should turn to the internal glands and organs, such as the heart and brain.

When one goes to bed one should ensure that one has completely "unwound" before going to sleep. If you are tense in your bed, you will remain tense throughout your sleep. But if you are relaxed at first, you will maintain that relaxation throughout the night, even though you change your position unconsciously while sleeping.

Part Five

19. SCHEDULE OF COURSES

FOR MEN AND WOMEN

IMPORTANT POINTS TO REMEMBER

In order to derive the maximum benefits from these exercises, it is necessary to co-ordinate the movements of muscles, with proper concentration and breathing. In your daily routine, first do the *āsana-s,* then practice relaxation, and then breathing. Relaxation may also be practiced for a few seconds between each two exercises.

The best times for yoga practice are before breakfast and supper; or you could practice two to three hours after a main meal. Soft drinks like fruit juice or milk may be had before or after the exercises. After light meals of fruit and milk, or other light food which does not contain concentrated starch or protein, they may be practiced an hour or a couple of hours later.

The exercises listed here have been selected as the best possible combination for the development of different parts of the body and mind. But it is not necessary that you should do them all on one and the same day. If you should give more time to one exercise, you should omit others or curtail the time for them, and do those which were omitted the following day.

These exercises are not tiring, nor do they strain the body. They may therefore be safely practiced when you are tired after a hard day's work. Regularity in practice is an important factor, but you may take a day off once every week or fortnight. But never get to feel that you are a slave to the routine. Whenever you feel in excellent health, you may forgo it for a day or two.

Always use some common sense and discrimination, and see that you do not strain. You may always make slight alterations about the time for exercising, and on the question of food. As to the latter it is better to use meat and eggs sparingly, if at all. The same applies to vinegar, common salt, pickles and pungent condiments.

Advanced students should not neglect the practice of "virtues" like forgiveness, contentment, selfless service and cleanliness of one's thoughts. These virtues are easily cultivated, if one first eradicates such evils as jealousy, anger, hatred and covetousness. Occasional fasting is good for advanced students since it helps in physical, mental and spiritual rejuvenation.

Non-injury in thought, deed and action is the highest virtue. This virtue could influence the whole world.

The practice of yoga breathing disciplines the life currents in the body so that they get in harmony with the Universal Spirit. After disciplining the body by the postures and breathing exercises, concentrate on *pratyāhāra* which is the science of bringing sensory organs under control through discrimination and self-enquiry. By control of the senses, one stops the outgoing tendency of the mind, which travels outwards through the senses like the rays of the sun, and tends to dissipate itself.

By practice of *pratyāhāra* and meditation these outgoing rays which emanate from the mind are controlled and focussed inside for self analysis and self study.

While doing these exercises, the room should be properly ventilated and one should wear as few clothes as possible — for the West shorts or bathing suits are suitable. If clothing constricts the movement of muscles, it interferes with their proper stretching, contraction and relaxation.

Men and women who are beginners should practice the postures, breathing exercises and relaxation for 15 to 30 minutes daily.

Advanced students can increase the time to one hour or more.

Women may discontinue the postures during menstruation, but can continue the breathing, meditation and relaxation.

At least four to five minutes should be given to relaxation, both by beginners and the advanced students.

Table I: BEGINNERS' COURSE FOR WOMEN

YOGA EXERCISES	Minimum	Maximum	Increase per month up to maximum
1. The Posture of the Hare	5 sec.	1½ min.	1 min.
2. Exercising the Waist	Twice	5 times	Once
3. The Half Locust Posture	Once	3 times	Once
4. Exercising the Abdomen	Once	Twice	Once
5. The Half Fish Posture	10 sec.	30 sec.	15 sec.
6. The Half Spinal Twist I	10 sec.	1 min.	20 sec.
7. The Lion Posture	10 sec.	40 sec.	20 sec.
8. Posture for Relieving Gas from Intestines & Colon	30 sec.	3 min.	1 min.
9. Applying Transverse Pressure on the Spine	10 sec.	1 min.	30 sec.
CONCENTRATION			
10. Concentration	2 min.	5 min.	2 min.
11. Meditation	5 min.	10 min.	2 min.

Table II: MAIN COURSE FOR WOMEN

YOGA EXERCISES	Minimum	Maximum	Increase per month up to maximum
1. The Cobra Posture	30 sec.	5 min.	1 min.
2. The Locust Posture	30 sec.	3 min.	1 min.
3. The Pan-Physical Posture	1 min.	7 min.	2 min.
4. The Fish Posture	30 sec.	1½ min.	1 min.
5. The Half Spinal Twist II	30 sec.	2 min.	1 min.
6. The Triangle Posture	30 sec.	1½ min.	30 sec.
7. The Plough Posture	30 sec.	3 min.	1 min.
8. *Āsana* for Stretching the Posterior Muscles of the Body	10 sec.	2 min.	1 min.
9. The Hero Posture	1 min.	5 min.	2 min.
YOGA BREATHING			
10. Cleansing Breathing	1 min.	3 min.	2 min.
11. Positive Breathing	5 min.	7 min.	2 min.
12. Breathing to Calm the Mind	5 min.	10 min.	2 min.
13. *Prānāyāma*	5 min.	10 min.	5 min.
CONCENTRATION			
14. Concentration	5 min.	15 min.	5 min.
15. Meditation	10 min.	20 min.	5 min.

Table III: ADVANCED COURSE FOR WOMEN

YOGA EXERCISES	Minimum	Maximum	Increase per month up to maximum
1. Head Stand in Lotus Posture	2 sec.	5 min.	1 min.
2. The Full Spine Twist	10 sec.	30 sec.	20 sec.
3. Half Tortoise Posture	15 sec.	1 min.	30 sec.
4. The Tortoise Posture	10 sec.	2 min.	30 sec.
5. Head Stand in Lotus Posture II	2 sec.	5 min.	1 min.
6. Posture for Stretching the Thighs	1 sec.	1 min.	30 sec.
7. The Plough Posture II	1 min.	5 min.	2 min.
8. The Locked Lotus Posture	1 min.	5 min.	3 min.
9. The Noose Posture	1 min.	5 min.	3 min.
10. The Prosperous Pose	5 min.	30 min.	10 min.
YOGA BREATHING			
11. Cleansing Breathing	3 min.	5 min.	2 min.
12. Positive Breathing	10 min.	15 min.	2 min.
13. Breathing to Calm the Mind	10 min.	15 min.	2 min.
14. *Prānāyāma*	15 min.	20 min.	10 min.
CONCENTRATION			
15. Concentration	15 min.	20 min.	5 min.
16. Meditation	20 min.	30 min.	5 min.

Table IV: BEGINNERS' COURSE FOR MEN

YOGA EXERCISES	Minimum	Maximum	Increase per month up to maximum
1. The Posture of the Hare	30 sec.	2 min.	1 min.
2. Exercising the Waist	3 times	5 times	Once
3. The Half Locust Posture	Twice	3 times	Once
4. Exercising the Abdomen	Twice	3 times	Once
5. The Half Fish Posture	30 sec.	1 min.	30 sec.
6. The Half Spinal Twist I	30 sec.	1½ min.	1 min.
7. The Lion Posture	20 sec.	1 min.	40 sec.
8. Posture for Relieving Gas from Intestines & Colon	1 min.	3 min.	2 min.
9. Applying Transverse Pressure on the Spine	30 sec.	1 min.	30 sec.
CONCENTRATION			
10. Concentration	5 min.	7 min.	2 min.
11. Meditation	5 min.	10 min.	5 min.

Table V: MAIN COURSE FOR MEN

YOGA EXERCISES	Minimum	Maximum	Increase per month up to maximum
1. The Cobra Posture	30 sec.	5 min.	1 min.
2. The Locust Posture	30 sec.	5 min.	1 min.
3. The Pan-Physical Posture	3 min.	10 min.	5 min.
4. The Fish Posture	30 sec.	2 min.	1 min.
5. The Half Spinal Twist II	1 min.	2 min.	1 min.
6. The Triangle Posture	1 min.	2 min.	1 min.
7. The Plough Posture	1 min.	3 min.	2 min.
8. *Āsana* for Stretching the Posterior Muscles of the Body	30 sec.	3 min.	2 min.
9. The Hero Posture	5 min.	15 min.	10 min.
YOGA BREATHING			
10. Cleansing Breathing	3 min.	5 min.	2 min.
11. Positive Breathing	7 min.	10 min.	3 min.
12. Breathing to Calm the Mind	10 min.	15 min.	5 min.
13. *Prānāyāma*	15 min.	20 min.	5 min.
CONCENTRATION			
14. Concentration	10 min.	20 min.	10 min.
15. Meditation	15 min.	30 min.	15 min.

Table VI: ADVANCED COURSE FOR MEN

YOGA EXERCISES	Minimum	Maximum	Increase per month up to maximum
1. Head Stand in Lotus Posture	3 min.	5 min.	2 min.
2. The Full Spine Twist	30 sec.	1½ min.	1 min.
3. Half Tortoise Posture	1 min.	3 min.	2 min.
4. The Tortoise Posture	1 min.	4 min.	3 min.
5. Head Stand in Lotus Posture II	5 min.	10 min.	2 min.
6. Posture for Stretching the Thighs	2 min.	5 min.	3 min.
7. The Plough Posture	3 min.	10 min.	2 min.
8. The Locked Lotus Posture	2 min.	5 min.	2 min.
9. The Noose Posture	2 min.	5 min.	3 min.
10. The Prosperous Pose	10 min.	30 min.	20 min.
YOGA BREATHING			
11. Cleansing Breathing	5 min.	10 min.	5 min.
12. Positive Breathing	15 min.	20 min.	5 min.
13. Breathing to Calm the Mind	15 min.	20 min.	5 min.
14. *Prānāyāma*	20 min.	30 min.	10 min.
CONCENTRATION			
15. Concentration	15 min.	30 min.	5 min.
16. Meditation	20 min.	30 min.	10 min.

INDEX

157

160

CPSIA information can be obtained at www.ICGtesting.com
Printed in the USA
LVOW11s1227230414

382885LV00006BA/254/P